FOOTBALL APPRENTICES

FOOTBALL APPRENTICES
David Holman

Cambridge University Press

CAMBRIDGE
LONDON   NEW YORK   NEW ROCHELLE
MELBOURNE   SYDNEY

ACT NOW PLAYS

Series editor: Andrew Bethell

Roots, Rules and Tribulation   Andrew Bethell
Closed Circuit   Mike English
Faust and Furious   Anne Lee
Czechmate   Gerry Docherty and Bill Kinross
Spring Offensive   Ray Speakman and Derek Nicholls
Football Apprentices   David Holman

Published by the Press Syndicate of the University of Cambridge
The Pitt Building, Trumpington Street, Cambridge CB2 1RP
32 East 57th Street, New York, NY 10022, USA
296 Beaconsfield Parade, Middle Park, Melbourne 3206, Australia

© Cambridge University Press 1982

First published 1982

Printed in Great Britain by David Green Printers Ltd

ISBN 0 521 28567 4 paperback

Performance
For permission to give a public performance of *Football Apprentices* please write to Permissions Department, Cambridge University Press, The Edinburgh Building, Shaftesbury Road, Cambridge CB2 2RU.

ABOUT THE PLAY

Professional football may seem like a glamorous career, but the glamour is only half the story. Every year thousands of sixteen-year-old boys are flattered into joining football clubs as apprentices, convinced that they will be the ones to 'make it to the top'. For most of them, it is a waste of time; aged eighteen, they are unceremoniously dumped by their clubs, two years older and two years behind in the job queue.

Football Apprentices is a play about what happens to boys who set their sights on the professional game. It shows how they become involved, the sacrifices they must make, their hopes and their disappointments. There is nothing glamorous about the experience of Walcott Burns, a black midfield player, and Clive Pope, a small goalkeeper. At school they thought they were good; when approached by the club they have no doubts – but neither of them is prepared for the pressures that follow. Parents, teachers, senior players, coaches and fellow apprentices all have their say, but in the end it is the manager who decides whether they are to be signed or not. He has his own worries, which do not leave much room for sympathy and understanding.

Football Apprentices was specially written for the Theatre Royal, Stratford, in East London (located halfway between Orient and West Ham), and the production included a group of local schoolboys. The writer and director spent months researching the subject, and the end result was considered realistic enough to be used in a BBC documentary. There is plenty to laugh at, but the play also provokes a lot of serious questions about how responsible football clubs are in their search for cheap young talent.

Football Apprentices will appeal to any group of young people who follow football. It will be of particular interest to those who might be tempted to follow Walcott and Clive.

CHARACTERS

Schoolboy football players (later to be apprentices)

WALCOTT BURNS   A black midfielder
CLIVE POPE   A goalkeeper
MICKY FIELDER   a midfielder
HENRY HOLT   a left-back
JOHN MITCHELL   a central defender

Other schoolboys

KEITH SANDERSON
DEAN MARSHALL
DOUGLAS SMITH

IAN ANDERSON   the club's assistant manager
PETE MILLER   youth team coach
ALAN BOYD   a first-team player
FRANK FORD   an apprentice goalkeeper
MR POPE
MRS POPE
MR MCNAB   a teacher
EDDIE QUINN   manager

STAGE DIRECTIONS

There are two kinds of directions in this playscript. Those in **bold type** provide information that is essential to an understanding of what is happening in the play at that time. For a play-reading, these should be read by a separate reader.

Those in *italic type* are less essential stage directions and offer suggestions to assist with a production of the play on stage. In a reading they are best not read out as they will hamper the flow of the play, although those who are reading may find that some of these instructions offer help with the interpretation of their lines.

ACT ONE

SCENE 1   A Second Division football club in East London: the home dressing room. It is a Saturday morning, after the youth team have played a South-East Counties match against Norwich City. There are five players: WALCOTT BURNS, CLIVE POPE, MICKY FIELDER, HENRY HOLT and JOHN MITCHELL. **Walcott Burns and Clive Pope are standing apart from the others, combing their hair and putting on ties. The others are still changing from the game.**

JOHN   Five-one!

WALCOTT   *(Combing hair and looking at himself in the mirror)* Marius Tresor!*

JOHN   Five-one at home! Ian's going to roast us.

MICKY   Pete already has.

CLIVE   *(Combing hair also)* Shilton!

MICKY   Why did he have to come this week? We were good last week.

JOHN   We could have held 'em to two-one or three-one if that flash sod hadn't got himself sent off.

MICKY   Leave it out, John. He's going to get enough aggravation from Ian.

WALCOTT   We'd have held 'em to one-one if we had a goalkeeper who wasn't a daffodil.

HENRY   Daffodil?

*Black French international player, outstanding in 1978 World Cup Finals in Argentina.

WALCOTT   Comes out once a year. Three crosses. Three goals. *(Back to combing)* Tresor!

JOHN   You just want your mate in goal, don't you flash?

WALCOTT   All right, you're a centre back. Who would you sooner have behind you, him or Frankie? Come on, you got all the mouth. Him or Frankie Ford? *(To Clive)* You'll be in next week.

JOHN   He might be and you know what you'll be doing? Watching the 'Multi-coloured Swap Shop' Saturday morning. He ain't going to choose you again. Sent off for chinning a spectator! Cor dear!

WALCOTT   It was a push! That's all. Poxy ref!

MICKY   Oh hello, Ref!

WALCOTT   *(After falling for it and glaring at Micky, turns to Clive.)* You'll be in next week.

CLIVE   He can't chuck out an apprentice for me.

WALCOTT   Clive, you're a better keeper. I don't know how you stand it. Sitting on the bench every week just hoping Frankie breaks a leg or lets in ten. I wouldn't take that.

CLIVE   I don't.

WALCOTT   You show me a substitute who wants his team to play well and I'll show you a liar.

MICKY   All right. All right. Who's got my kipper?

JOHN   I don't know.

MICKY   Nobody leaves till I got my kipper.

JOHN   Come on, Ian! Get it over with.

CLIVE   *(To Walcott)* What did that bloke say to you at the throw-in?

WALCOTT   Forget it.

CLIVE   What did he say?

WALCOTT He says . . . well you saw him doing that to me *(indicating gorilla action)* when I was his side of the field. Then at the throw-in he says: 'You do the PG Tips, don't you?'

JOHN <u>Wallop</u>.

MICKY All right, who's the comedian? My girlfriend gave me that tie.

CLIVE You looking for the blue one?

MICKY Yes. You seen it?

CLIVE No.

JOHN <u>She give you that, did she? Can't think a lot of you</u>.

(Enter PETE MILLER, the youth team coach, with the apprentice goalkeeper, FRANK FORD, still in full match kit.)

PETE *(To Frank)* Go on, son, hurry up and get showered. Don't worry about it, son. *(Looks at Walcott.)* Walcott Burns! *(Shakes his head.)*

JOHN <u>Played, Frankie</u>.

PETE Ian only wants to see our schools players in here, Frankie, so hurry it up. He's seeing the apprentices in the First Team dressing room after.

MICKY How long's Ian going to be, Pete? My club match starts at two.

PETE Not long. He's talking to Brownie and Boydie.

JOHN <u>Oh Christ, were they watching an' all?</u>

PETE Yeah, your first-team stars come and watch the team that I trained, and do you perform up to your potential, or do you show me up? You know I'm getting the sack Monday 'cause of you lot.

MICKY Did Ian see all the game?

HENRY What did he think of me, Pete?

JOHN <u>What did he think, Pete</u>?

PETE   He'll tell you. Anyone want some ointment to put on their ears to save the burns?

JOHN   Didn't he like anything about it?

PETE   He liked the final whistle. You didn't do too bad, some of you.

HENRY   Who?

MICKY   Pete, someone's got my kipper.

PETE   John Mitchell. *(John goes to get the tie.)* Right. Expenses. Who hasn't had 'em yet?

(John Mitchell has the tie. It is wet. Walcott and Henry come to sign the expenses form. Pete has a see-through bag of silver.)

MICKY   Oh look at this. My girlfriend gave me this. It's all wet, and I'm seeing her tonight.

CLIVE   Bad luck with that penalty, Frank.

JOHN   Are you still going out with that Michelle?

MICKY   Yeah.

JOHN   Henry thinks she looks like one of them in 'Charlie's Angels'.

MICKY   Do you?

HENRY   Yeah.

MICKY   Which one, as a matter of interest?

JOHN   Charlie!

PETE   *(Looking at the expenses form)* Walcott, you don't live near the ground. How come you put down 20p each way expenses to get here? Frankie, come on, son.

WALCOTT   That's what I give 'em.

PETE   Give who?

WALCOTT   The Tube.

PETE   Tube? Your fare's got to be a quid single from where you live.

WALCOTT That's what I give 'em: 20p.

PETE Give who?

WALCOTT Whoever's on the gate.

PETE Look, Walcott, I don't know whether I'm going to need to tell you this because you may not need to travel to the club after your exhibition today but . . .

WALCOTT Is that what Ian said?

PETE He'll tell you. But if you do come again on the Tube . . . ain't you ever heard of the railway police? They could come down here in the middle of a match and arrest you. We're *in loco parentis* with you, son. I'm giving you two quid. Pay the full fare.

WALCOTT OK.

MICKY All right. All right. Who's got my shoes? Pete!

PETE Look for 'em, Micky Fielder.

MICKY They're twenty-five quid shoes, Pete.

PETE Them coloured things?

MICKY They're Adam Ant shoes.

PETE You shouldn't wear other boys' shoes. It's bad for your feet.

(Enter ALAN BOYD, an experienced first-team player, dressed in very smart, casual clothes. The youth players greet him with respect. Frank has been ready to go into the shower, but it's him that Boyd wants to see.)

BOYD Just have a word, Frank, before the coach goes. That penalty, son. I'm not getting at you, you made some good saves, but why did you go right for that penalty?

FRANK I don't know.

BOYD *(To Clive)* You're a goalkeeper an' all. What's your name?

CLIVE Clive Pope.

BOYD   Popey, you come here an' all. *(To Frank)* Now I'm not getting at you. You don't know why you went right for that penalty?

FRANK   No.

BOYD   What were you watching on his run-up? Body? Legs? Head?

FRANK   Position of the body.

BOYD   Is that what you'd do, Popey?

CLIVE   Yes.

PETE   What do you know about goalkeeping, Boydie?

BOYD   Right, Frank, you're in goal. I'm moving in for a penalty. *(Does this in slow motion.)* My leading foot starts to go down. Right. Which way is that ball going to go? It can only go one way, can't it? There. That's the natural movement. Now if I put my foot there, then it's got to go there. Clive Pope, you an' all, watch run-ups, get people to run towards you. You've got a split second when that foot's committed and that tells you which way you've got to go. 'Course some are so good that that split second's no good to you. Practise it.

(Ian Anderson comes in at the door. There is a definite reaction from the youth players.)

IAN   Alan Boyd. The first-team coach is waiting.

BOYD   Right, Ian.

JOHN   Best of luck at Millwall, Boydie! *(Echoed by the others.)*

IAN   *(Taking Boyd out)* I'll see you over there. I'm going by car. I'll be in to see you schoolboys in thirty seconds.

(Ian and Boyd go out.)

MICKY   Oh Christ, I still can't find my shoes, Pete.

PETE   Come on, into the shower, Frankie. And you lot, let's get this kit cleared up. Our reserves are in here this afternoon, and I don't want them sitting in this mess.

HENRY   What did you think of my game, Pete? You didn't say
          nothing after the match.

PETE   I've given my rollocking. You don't want any more, do
          you? Listen, Henry, you had a good game. You know
          your only trouble, son? You're a quiet boy. You don't
          shout for the ball. Three times you went on overlaps when
          Micky Fielder had the ball. Three times you went up the
          field and three times you didn't shout to tell him you
          were there. You ran a thousand yards up and down that
          line today and you didn't get that ball once because you
          didn't give him information. You didn't tell him you
          were there. This is a hard game when you haven't got
          options, son, and you're not an option for the man with
          the ball if he don't know you're there. You might make a
          wonderful marathon runner, Henry, but you'll never be a
          footballer until you learn to shout.

JOHN   Quit shaking, Walcott. It'll soon be over.

WALCOTT   Get lost.

PETE   Now, have I got all your gear in here?

          (The youth players nod and wait.)

MICKY   Come on. Who's got my shoes?

          (No answer. The youth players wait. Ian enters.)

IAN   Right! I know you've all got club games to get to. All of
          you? *(All the youth players nod.)* Right, so we've been
          beaten five–one by Norwich City youth. I don't mind
          losing. I don't even mind losing five-one. Norwich are a
          First Division club; you're playing a side that's bigger and
          older than you. Norwich are fielding eight or nine full
          apprentices: our side's mainly schools players. I don't
          mind losing to a side like that if I get 110 per cent effort
          from my players. Where's Steven Dean and Barry?

PETE   They had to go to their club games.

IAN   Pity. 110 per cent effort! I didn't get that! I got seventy
          minutes out of you, Micky Fielder, And that's no bloody

good to me. Your head was on your chest for the last
twenty minutes. You threw in the towel, didn't you?
Didn't you?

MICKY Yes.

IAN I'm not interested in seventy-minute players I want ninety
or you're out! Right? Right?

MICKY Yes.

IAN Henry, I called you a coward after the Ipswich game. Am
I going to repeat that after today's match? Eh? What do
you think? In that Ipswich match you didn't get in a
tackle after we went two down. I was proud of you today,
son. That's the best winger you've had to cope with all
season. He skinned you for half an hour but you came
back at him, you closed him down and he was ineffectual
in the last half hour. Good. I wish some of the other
yellow streaks in this team had disappeared like that
today.

PETE I told him about the shouting.

IAN Henry, I want you to want that ball so badly that you're
shouting for the whole ninety minutes. I want you to
sound like Windsor Davies. Shout at me!

HENRY What?

IAN Anything.

HENRY Geronimo!

IAN Louder!

HENRY Geronimo!!

IAN John Mitchell, what time did you go to bed last night?

JOHN Early.   You looked half dead out

IAN What were you doing? Playing with yourself?   face

JOHN No.

IAN What?

JOHN I had a school match last night.

IAN   On a Friday night? What do they mean having matches when you're wanted here on Saturday mornings?

JOHN   House match.

IAN   Take 'em in a note. I want you resting Friday night. Tell 'em you can't make it. I don't want knackered central defenders in this standard of football. I want you to work with Pete Tuesday night when you come in on your defensive heading. OK, Pete? Right now . . . Walcott, I want to see you when the others have gone . . . and you, Clive Pope. Right, now all of you listen. This is important. There are eight games left before the end of the season.

(**Frank comes through from the shower.**)

Frankie, take your stuff through and change in the First Team dressing room. I'm coming in to see the APs* in five minutes. On you go, son, and cheer up! It's not the end of the world. I was in a team that lost nine–one once.

(**Frank goes off, receiving sympathetic looks from some of the schools players.**)

We've got eight games for you to prove yourselves. During that time the manager, Gordon, in consultation with me as assistant and the youth-team coach here, will make a choice about which of the schools players we're going to offer apprentice forms. Eight games! If you want to play professional football for us, you'd better get your fingers out, or this club won't be signing any apprentices this year. I mean it. You've got everything to do.

JOHN   Excuse me. Is Gordon coming to see us, then?

IAN   He's coming next week to see you play Spurs. Don't get frightened just 'cause the manager's coming to see you. Spurs is a good club. We're not expecting miracles. 110 per cent. If we get that, you'll be all right. Don't worry about Gordon.

*Apprentices.

JOHN   <u>Christ!</u>

IAN   Ninety minutes. Right, off to your school games. Enjoy
'em; you're all stars in those teams, big fish in your little
pools. Here, you're wearing L-plates. And those that
aren't prepared to learn can piss off. Right. See you
Tuesday night for training. Away you go.

MICKY   Pete, I still haven't got my shoes.

IAN   Give him his shoes.

**(John quickly finds the shoes in a hiding place, and the youth
players start to leave. As they do so, MR POPE comes in.)**

MR POPE   Sorry, Ian, is Clive ready? I'm driving him to his club
match. Hello, Pete.

PETE   Hello, Mr Pope.

IAN   Can you give me a couple of minutes, Mr Pope?

MR POPE   Yes. And I'm taking Walcott as well.

IAN   A couple of minutes then.

MR POPE   Coventry City has invited Clive up there for a week to
look around. See if they like each other. They seem very
keen.

IAN   Good. I'll have him with you in a couple of minutes.

(Mr Pope goes off with a signal to Clive to hurry it up.)

IAN   Are you fit, Clive Pope?

CLIVE   Yes, sir.

IAN   You want to play against Spurs next week?

CLIVE   Yes, sir.

IAN   Ian.

CLIVE   Yes, sir.

IAN   This is the big one, Clive. Can you grow two inches by
next week?

CLIVE   Yes, sir Ian. Well I . . .

IAN   That's OK. It'll come. What do you think about taking an apprentice goalkeeper's place next week?

CLIVE   I don't know.

IAN   What?

CLIVE   I don't know.

IAN   Clive! Clive! You're a goalkeeper. Goalkeepers are positive. They're decisive. I don't want a shrinking violet as my goalkeeper. I want a man. I want men at sixteen. So I want you to think positively: 'Right Spurs, I'm Clive Pope and you're not going to get a smell today.' Right?

CLIVE   Yes, sir.

IAN   You model yourself on Shilton, don't you?

CLIVE   Yes, sir.

IAN   He dominates his area; that's what I want from you. OK Shilton, see you Tuesday night.

CLIVE   *(Going)* Right. *(To Walcott)* I'll wait for you outside.

(Clive goes off. Walcott is left alone with Pete and Ian. There is a long pause as Ian looks at Walcott.)

IAN   You big, stupid . . . When was the last time we had a player sent off?

PETE   We never have.

IAN   What did that spectator say to you? No, I don't want to know what he said. It doesn't matter what he said. You lost us that game, Walcott Burns. We were one–one when you lost your bottle. Do you think you're the first coloured who's taken a bit of stick? You know how you answer that. Not by throwing punches. The way Viv Anderson answers it, the way Chiedozie answers it, the way Regis answers it. By being a bloody good player. If you play League football there's plenty of grounds where they're going to give you the gorilla. Newcastle, Middlesbrough, plenty of places. If you can't take that you're no good to us. You're a stupid, flashy sod. I'm not talking about your play. Character! You've got good skills, you've got a brain, but you've never played for a team, you've never won a fifty–fifty ball in your life. That is going to change. *(Pause)* I *was* going to tell you next week, but I'm going to tell you now, so you can think over all the implications. Gordon wants to sign you apprentice professional. But before that happens I want you to take a little while and have a good long think. If you sign you'll be working with me and Peter Miller. Our job will be to turn you from a flash schools playboy, who doesn't know which end is up, into a team player we can use. If you want an easy life, don't sign. OK. Go on, Mr Pope's waiting for you.

(Walcott looks at him and then charges out.)

WALCOTT   *(Off)* TRESOR!!

IAN   Birk! *(Pause)* Good first half, Pete.

PETE   I was pleased with Henry.

IAN   Young Frank's in a state.

PETE   Yes. If you had Clive's ability and Frankie's height, you'd have a cracking keeper.

IAN   Clive'll grow.

PETE   I hope so. Five foot eight isn't much good to us.

IAN   *(Going)* We can build on that first half.

(They go out.)

SCENE 2   A classroom in a local comprehensive school for boys. Kids are banging on their desks. These are KEITH SANDERSON, DEAN MARSHALL and DOUGLAS SMITH.

(WALCOTT enters with his football bag.)

KEITH   You're in the wrong spot, Walcott. This ain't a betting shop.

WALCOTT   I don't know you, do I?

DOUGLAS   *(Pointing to book)* Where did we get up to in this?

KEITH	You're getting very flash just because some rat-bag club asked you to put an *X* on their form, ain't you?
WALCOTT	Who is he?
DEAN	What you doing here, Walcott?
WALCOTT	*(Holding up bag)* School match.
DOUGLAS	Where we got to in this revision?
DEAN	Causes of the First World War.
DOUGLAS	Who's got notes on this?
KEITH	Get your own notes, Smiff.

(Dean hands Douglas a note book.)

WALCOTT	Where's McNab? He's paid to be here.

(Enter CLIVE. He and Walcott slap hands. Then Clive gets out his hand-exercisers.)

CLIVE	Simmo says to tell you why haven't you been up to see him.
WALCOTT	I don't need to see him. I already got a career. Anyway, I know London Transport's number. What did he say to you? Does he think you'll pass?
CLIVE	He expects me to get five.
KEITH	Simmo's always been an optimist.
CLIVE	I says footballer first choice, and he keeps saying, 'What's your second choice?'
WALCOTT	Complete waste of time. Know what he said to me last time I went? 'Walcott, what have you ever done for this school?'
KEITH	Good question.
CLIVE	Leave it out, Sanderson. Get on with your knitting.
WALCOTT	Thank you, brother. I says, 'How do you think this school got to the semi-final of the London cup? You ask Tulse Hill what I done for this school.' 'Academically', he says. 'Academically', I says, 'Simmo', I says, 'don't talk to me about academically. Desist', I says.

DOUGLAS   Dean, your writing's terrible. What does that say after 'France'?

DEAN   *Entente cordiale.*

DOUGLAS   With a *K*? Is that right?

DEAN   It's French.

WALCOTT   Douglas, we're talking. *(Turns on Douglas like a teacher.)* Russo-Japanese War?

DOUGLAS   1905.

WALCOTT   1904. McNab wouldn't last long at Fords with this timekeeping, would he? *(To Clive)* Training hard for the Spurs, Clive?

CLIVE   Yeah.

WALCOTT   I thought you was. I thought I saw you over the park during school hours.

CLIVE   Shut up!

WALCOTT   I'll give you a run out tomorrow. Practice on penalties and crosses and that.

CLIVE   I don't know.

WALCOTT   Come on! Here Douglas, what Simmo recommend you by way of a career?

DOUGLAS   Army.

KEITH   Thank Christ we got a navy.

DOUGLAS   There's lots of water-skiing in Germany.

WALCOTT   Lots of graves in Belfast an' all. It wouldn't cost much for your coffin, Douglas. Get you in a Swan's matchbox. Paris Commune?

DOUGLAS   1871.

WALCOTT   *(To Clive)* Here, about Saturday, you did want Frankie Ford to let in ten, didn't you?

CLIVE   Nine.

(Enter MR MCNAB, **putting his jacket on.**)

MCNAB Sorry, lads. Swimming-pool boiler again. OK, 5.3.

WALCOTT I should think so, sir. Tax payers' money.

MCNAB Sorry, I don't think I recognise you. New boy?

WALCOTT Very funny, sir. Least I'm here.

MCNAB *(Throwing lunchtime newspaper)* That affect you?

CLIVE What is it?

WALCOTT They sacked Gordon last night.

CLIVE Blimey!

WALCOTT *(Reading)* Ian's been made acting manager. Oh Christ.

MCNAB Read it afterwards. Not a very gentlemanly act with still a good chance of avoiding the drop. Still, as the poet Coleman would say, 'That's football.' However, today, 5.3, my little band of brothers who stand like greyhounds in the slips . . .

DEAN Three slips, two short legs, sir.

MCNAB I do the jokes, Marshall. Today's revision is revision of revision, so I expect this to be sharp and right. We will be dealing with, among other things, the dropping of another eminent First Division manager, Otto von Bismark. Causes of the First World War. Sanderson, thank you. I know you're looking forward to causing the Third World War, but if I can have your razor-sharp intellect focussed here. Sanderson, these brown smudges on the European map, achieved, if I may say so, by a born artist, myself, are what, Sanderson?

(This revision lesson should be carried through at high speed. Either they know it or they are quickly consulting notes under the desks.)

KEITH Hills, sir.

MCNAB More grandiose, Sanderson.

KEITH Mountains.

MCNAB   Yes, very important to the political make-up of Europe in the days before aircraft – mountains. Am I keeping you up, Pope? Get Pope some Horlicks. These countries are, Douglas?

DOUGLAS   Austria-Hungary, sir.

MCNAB   Try it without Marshall's notes, Douglas. This?

DOUGLAS   Prussia.

MCNAB   Led from 1852 by!

KEITH   Otto von Bismark.

MCNAB   His boss?

DEAN   Wilhelm the First.

MCNAB   Altogether! Title?

ALL   Kaiser!!

MCNAB   Good. What makes it likely that these two will become allies? Reel off a dozen reasons.

CLIVE   No natural barriers.

MCNAB   Not out of the window, Marshall. Yes.

DEAN   Same language.

DOUGLAS   Same religion.

MCNAB   Result in 1879?

DOUGLAS   Dual alliance.

MCNAB   Good. *Dual* meaning *two*, Walcott. Bismark then turns his attention here.

CLIVE   Russia.

MCNAB   And achieves a further alliance called?

KEITH   Three Emperors League.

MCNAB   German?

CLIVE   *Drei Kaiser Bund.*

MCNAB   Russian Emperor called?

KEITH	Tsar.
MCNAB	Good, Tsar Nicholas. Something interesting outside the window, Walcott? Not your type, Walcott. Tsar Nicholas. Not someone we would have spent too much time on had it not been for the way he met his end. How, Sanderson?
KEITH	They got a crew out, sir.
MCNAB	Pardon?
KEITH	He had a contract out on him, sir.
MCNAB	From whom?
WALCOTT	From whom?
KEITH	Commies, sir.
MCNAB	Anarchists, Sanderson. There is difference. Among the hit-men?
DOUGLAS	Lenin's brother, sir.
MCNAB	Lenin's full name?
KEITH	Vladimir Ilich Ulyanov, sir.
MCNAB	Who was to have some little influence later on. Don't do that, Walcott, you'll go blind. Three Emperors League aimed at which country in particular?
CLIVE	Don't know, sir.
MCNAB	You should know this stuff, Clive Pope. We've been through this a dozen times. France, boy.
CLIVE	I do know it, sir.
MCNAB	You don't. You should know all of it. France isolated. However, back to these two. One fly in the Clearasil as far as these two are concerned, Walcott?
WALCOTT	Yes, sir.
MCNAB	Still with us, Walcott?
WALCOTT	Yes, sir. Why don't you ask me something, sir?
MCNAB	Could I? Well, would you like to hazard a guess as to some long-term differences between these two countries?

WALCOTT   Between Russia and Austria-Hungary?
           (McNab nods.) Salonika?

MCNAB   Salonika is?

WALCOTT   The port that Russia wanted and Austria didn't want her
           to have.

MCNAB   Russia's got plenty of ports, Walcott. Reel off a couple up
           here, Pope. *(No answer)* All right, Douglas.

DOUGLAS   Murmansk and Archangel.

MCNAB   Not from Marshall's notes, Douglas, thank you. Plenty of
           ports, Walcott.

WALCOTT   Yeah, but those freeze over in the football season, sir.

MCNAB   Winter, I think the period is known as, Walcott.

WALCOTT   They want a warm-water port, Sir.

MCNAB   Got warm-water ports. Here! Where, Pope? Douglas?

DOUGLAS   Black Sea.

MCNAB   Reel off a couple, Pope. Sanderson?

KEITH   Sebastapol.

DOUGLAS   Odessa, Sir.

MCNAB   Warm-water ports, Walcott!

WALCOTT   No good to 'em in a war, sir. Turkey controls the
           Dardanelles. Now you get hold of Salonika and your
           problems are over, but Austria-Hungary ain't going to
           like that 'cause that's her patch down there. Like
           Everton–Liverpool down there, sir.

           (The bell goes for the end of the lesson.)

MCNAB   Good, well we'll go on from there next time. All right,
           Walcott?

WALCOTT   When's that, sir?

MCNAB   Thursday.

WALCOTT   I don't think I'm available for that one, sir.

MCNAB   *(Keeping Walcott and Clive back)* On you go, the rest of
           you. Quietly!

(The other three boys clear all five desks during the following conversation.)

MCNAB   Walcott, you could get this subject.

WALCOTT   You carry on, sir. Nice lesson. *(Hands back his newspaper.)*

MCNAB   Walcott, a word of advice from a Fulham supporter. It's a greasy pole that game. *(Indicating newspaper)* They've signed you, congratulations, but don't get too flash just in case it doesn't work out. Keep a level head. On you go. Clive!

(Walcott goes a little way off.)

MCNAB   You've missed my last two lessons. What's the matter? Am I off form?

CLIVE   No, sir. Throat, sir.

MCNAB   Seems all right now.

CLIVE   Yes, sir.

MCNAB   How many nights are you out training, Clive?

CLIVE   Four.

MCNAB   You're going backwards, lad. I've got one word for you, Pope. Work. I don't want you looking back on these six months and regretting anything. What are those things?

CLIVE   They strengthen your hands, sir.

MCNAB   *(Tapping Clive's head)* That's what needs strengthening. On you go.

(McNab goes. Walcott comes back to Clive.)

WALCOTT   What did he say?

CLIVE   Work and don't bunk off. It's all right for him, he ain't playing Spurs youth Saturday.

WALCOTT   Still want to come training tomorrow?

CLIVE   I'll see.

WALCOTT   I'm easy. They've signed me.

(They go off.)

SCENE 3   The Pope household. MRS POPE is reading the *Daily Mirror*.)

(CLIVE **comes home from school.**)

MRS POPE   That you, Clive?

CLIVE   *(Off)* Yes, Mum.

MRS POPE   The drain's blocked up again. *(As Clive enters)* How was school?

CLIVE   OK.

MRS POPE   I'll get your tea when your Dad comes in.

CLIVE   You done something to your hair, Mum?

MRS POPE   Yeah, what do you think?

CLIVE   It's all right.

MRS POPE   Anything you want for your tea?

CLIVE   Can I have something with protein in it?

MRS POPE   Hmmmm?

CLIVE   Protein. Shilton has lots of that.

MRS POPE   Oh yeah?

CLIVE   Cheese, eggs, fish, steaks.

MRS POPE   Well, I hope your mate Shilton's buying the steak then, the price of it. You can have a cheese sandwich.

CLIVE   I've got to grow, Mum.

MRS POPE   You can have two cheese sandwiches. *(About hair)* I don't know about this. You going out tonight?

CLIVE   Training.

MRS POPE   After?

CLIVE   No.

MRS POPE   Don't you never see what's-her-name no more?

CLIVE   No.

MRS POPE   What was the matter with her?

CLIVE	I don't know. *(Pause)* Mum?
MRS POPE	Hmmm?
CLIVE	Mum, how tall were Gran and Grandpa before they shrunk? They have, haven't they?
MRS POPE	Don't really think about it when you see 'em every week.
CLIVE	Were they taller when you were small?
MRS POPE	Well, they were to me, obviously!
CLIVE	What about Dad's side?
MRS POPE	Well, the husband was tall; the wife was titchy. She didn't like being called 'titchy'. She liked 'petite'.
CLIVE	You're five seven. Dad's five ten-and-a-half. I should be . . . it's that little woman on Dad's side.
MRS POPE	Clive, *che sera sera.* OK? Don't your football mates ever go on anywhere after?
CLIVE	Sometimes.
MRS POPE	What, discos?
CLIVE	Yeah.
MRS POPE	You don't fancy that?
CLIVE	No, Not really. Oh, I forgot this. From school. *(Hands her an envelope.)*
MRS POPE	Not another sponsored swim. 10p a length! Nobody told me that the school pool was twelve foot long!
CLIVE	It's a parents' meeting. About exams.
MRS POPE	What, you read this, have you?
CLIVE	No, someone opened theirs and I read that. You don't have to go, Mum. I'm doing all right.
MRS POPE	Oh yeah? Did the one you read have pen writing at the bottom?
CLIVE	*(Worried)* No. What?

MRS POPE   Who's written that?

CLIVE   McNab.

MRS POPE   What's this mean? . . . 'Attendance record affecting Clive's exam prospects.' What's that about?

CLIVE   I don't know.

MRS POPE   Clive, don't flannel me! What's it about?

CLIVE   A couple of half days.

MRS POPE   Doing what?

CLIVE   A bit of training.

MRS POPE   He wouldn't have written that for a couple of half days! Christ! It'll be those blokes coming round the door. Oh no. Oh no. Right.

(Mrs Pope goes off and comes back with a book.)

MRS POPE   You don't get enough training every night of the week? Right, there's your *Great Expectations*. Where you up to? Oh, congratulations: page eleven. Right mate, you get to page fifty and then you can have your tea. And I'm going to test you, and I've seen the film six times so I know what's in it.

CLIVE   What about my training, Mum?

MRS POPE   Your training's been cancelled.

CLIVE   I'm going. I'm playing Spurs Saturday.

MRS POPE   Maybe.

CLIVE   I am.

MRS POPE   Don't cheek me!

CLIVE   I'm not. I'm being positive.

MRS POPE   Well don't be positive like that or I'll clip your earhole. Read!!

(Clive reads. MR POPE enters. Happy.)

MRS POPE   No remarks about my hair. Thank you!

(Mr Pope looks at Clive and the book, puzzled.)

MRS POPE   And don't make no arrangements for next Wednesday night. We're going to a meeting down the school.

MR POPE   What's going on?

MRS POPE   And that drain's blocked again. Are you going down to phone the council emergency, or am I?

MR POPE   *(Checking watch)* Don't strain your eyes, son. You're going to be late for training.

MRS POPE   That's right. He's going to be very late for training. He ain't going.

MR POPE   He ain't injured? Not with Spurs Saturday.

MRS POPE   No, he's catching up on some school work he's missed 'cause he ain't been there.

MR POPE   Eh?

MRS POPE   Read that! *(To Clive)* Bedroom, you! What page you on? Go on.

(Clive goes and Mr Pope reads the letter.)

MRS POPE   Nice way you've brought up your son. Come in, Inspector!

MR POPE   Next Wednesday. Ahh.

MRS POPE   You're coming.

MR POPE   I wish you'd told me this yesterday.

MRS POPE   I'm telling you now.

MR POPE   *(About hair)* They done a nice job on that, Cath.

MRS POPE   You're coming.

MR POPE   Thing is, Pete's got me a couple of tickets for the away match with Orient next Wednesday. For me and Clive.

MRS POPE   Well Mr McNab's got me two tickets an' all. I'm talking about his studies.

MR POPE   What do you think I'm talking about? We're going down to study Mervyn Day behind the Orient goal. Come on, Cath, he's got to go training tonight. Gordon's watching him Saturday.

MRS POPE He's hopping off school; there's going to be inspectors coming round any minute; they're as good as saying he ain't going to get no bit of paper, and you're saying I'm going down there on me own next Wednesday to see McNab!!!

MR POPE No. No. Look, I'll come to the meeting. I'll skip the Orient match. I'll skip a six-pointer. But he's got to go to the ground tonight. It's make or break this week. Eh? I'll skip the Orient match. It's a six-pointer, Cath.

MRS POPE He's getting that bit of paper.

MR POPE Yeah.

MRS POPE So he does an hour's homework before he goes training, and we don't have the telly on when he comes back.

MR POPE OK. Except 'Sportsnight'.

MRS POPE Right.

MR POPE And the midweek match.

MRS POPE One or the other.

MR POPE *(Pause)* The match.

MRS POPE Right.

MR POPE Get changed, Clive! I'll drop you at the ground.

MRS POPE I'll make his tea and you phone the council about this drain on your way.

MR POPE They should have let this flat to Jack Hawkins. It's like the *Cruel Sea* with that sink. What time's this meeting? *(Checks letter.)* Why these schools can't check the fixture list before having a meeting, I don't know.

MRS POPE Clive! *Great Expectations*!

(They both go out.)

SCENE 4 **Parents night at the school. MR and MRS POPE are waiting in the classroom. Mr Pope has a transistor radio in his top pocket with an ear-piece. He is listening to the match reports.**

MRS POPE Alf?

MR POPE	One–nil to us. Fisher: own goal.

(He goes on listening as KEITH SANDERSON **enters.)**

KEITH	Mrs Pope?
MRS POPE	Yes.
KEITH	Mr McNab'll be with you in a sec. Some of the raffle prizes have walked.

(Keith goes off.)

MRS POPE	Take that out, Alf!
MR POPE	Sod it. Free kick to them. Just outside the box.
MRS POPE	Can't take you anywhere. Not much of a turn-out.
MR POPE	Well, they're not interested, are they? When I was here and they had a meeting you couldn't get in. 'Course, I think half of them only came for the tea and biscuits.
MRS POPE	Nice paintings.
MR POPE	Not much good if they can't read and write. That's the main thing. *(Pause)* Sod it!
MRS POPE	What?
MR POPE	They equalised. Henry Hughton.
MRS POPE	Take that out.

(MR MCNAB **enters.**)

MCNAB	Sorry to keep you. Nice to see you again. Mr Pope?
MRS POPE	Hello, Mr McNab.
MR POPE	Nice to meet you. I usually work evenings, see.
MCNAB	Right then. Clive.
MR POPE	Just saying. Nice paintings. Any of these Clive's?
MCNAB	No, I don't think so. No.
MRS POPE	How's Clive doing then, Mr McNab? Not too good?
MCNAB	To be frank, Mrs Pope, he appears to be going backwards . . . I mean that's not uncommon in the fourth and fifth years but . . .

MR POPE	Well, they want to get out to work, don't they?
MCNAB	Eighteen months ago I thought we might be talking about 'O' levels, maybe even 'A' levels. But the way he's going at the moment he's going to have to pull his socks up to get moderate CSEs.
MRS POPE	Christ, that bad? Well, it's his attendance record, is it?
MCNAB	No, it's his attitude.
MR POPE	Attitude? The club says he has a good attitude.
MCNAB	I'm sure they do. I'm competing with that club for his time and interest. They're winning.
MR POPE	He does some homework.
MRS POPE	At gunpoint.
MR POPE	Well, it is going to be his profession.
MCNAB	Is it?
MR POPE	Oh yes. They've as good as said so.
MCNAB	What if it doesn't work out, Mr Pope? Look, I had a couple of lads here who signed apprentice forms. West Ham was one and . . . what was the other one . . . Southend, I think it was. Both out on the street at eighteen. Now, it didn't bother the West Ham one. I think he'd got fed up with it anyway. The Southend boy, as far as I know, hasn't even started picking up the pieces yet. And that's a year ago. No qualifications, either of them.
MRS POPE	That's right.
MCNAB	With a couple of million unemployed, what are their chances?
MR POPE	Yes, but I could give you a couple of names of boys who are earning twice as much as you are. See what I mean? No, if Clive can put on another couple of inches, they've got no doubts about him.
MCNAB	Mr Pope, of course they are going to say that. But how many go on? Forty per cent? Thirty per cent?

MR POPE   You want him to forget football?

MCNAB   I don't believe in miracles, Mr Pope.

MR POPE   So what are you saying?

MRS POPE   Alf!

MR POPE   We know it's a risk, but if he makes it he'll have something neither you nor me have got, Mr McNab.

MCNAB   What's that?

MRS POPE   Alf, don't be cheeky.

MCNAB   It's all right. Yes, Mr Pope?

MR POPE   He'll be a name. And he won't have to live in a council flat where you can only live if you're a trained swimmer.

MRS POPE   It's not that bad.

MR POPE   It's all right if you're Jack Cousteau. Do you know what I dream, Mr McNab? I'm at Wembley in a seat. People all around me are saying things like 'Butch and Trevor are a bit off today, but Clive's keeping them out. Clive's breaking those forwards' hearts.' Not Clive Pope, but Clive, like you'd say Bobby or Dennis or Pat. I mean, you could take a canoe up the Amazon and shout out 'Bobby', and they'd shout back: 'Which one? Charlton or Moore?'

MRS POPE   You see what I mean with him, Mr McNab?

MR POPE   It's all right, Cath, we're having a conversation here. You'll agree that could happen?

MCNAB   Yes, it could. And what could also happen is that that club would get shot of Clive in eighteen months time. Eighteen years old and nothing.

MR POPE   Not nothing, Mr McNab, because he'll know. He had his chance and he didn't make it. Clive isn't going to come home and tell me I didn't give him every encouragement.

MCNAB   He'll be eighteen, two years behind on the job market, and what if he reacts like that Southend boy of mine?

MR POPE   He'll be able to take that.

MCNAB   But how would you take it, Mr Pope?

MR POPE   You're not getting my point.

MRS POPE   Alf, don't be cheeky.

MR POPE   It's all right, Cath. He says it's all right. Look, I had a
choice once. Go on and get some qualifications, or keep a
band together. A steady job, or living off crisps and a
prayer on talent competitions, hoping some night an
agent would walk in and like what we played.

MRS POPE   He hasn't got time for this.

MR POPE   Have you? *(Mr McNab indicates that he might have.)* And we
were good. You heard of a band called The High
Numbers? We were on the same bill with 'em once.

MCNAB   No, I don't . . .

MR POPE   You might know the name they took later on: 'The
Who'? We were on the same bill with them. They went
on, we packed it in.

MRS POPE   We're here to talk about Clive.

MR POPE   I *am* talking about Clive. I had my fantasies. I never
followed 'em. Gene Vincent, Eddie Cochrane, Chuck
Berry, Johnny Lafontaine. That was my stage name. Do
you know how we spent our wedding evening? Chasing
Gene Vincent up the A1 on my motor bike, with her on
the back . . . that was our wedding reception, taking our
mates to his show. One of 'em sent a card round to Gene
and he was gracious enough to play *Rocky Road Blues* for
us. He made the tribute from the stage: Johnny
Lafontaine, a fellow rock-and-roller, and his bride.

MRS POPE   Alf!

MR POPE   Clive didn't want to know the drums. A football, that's
all he wanted. Football. Shilton. Shilton eats this. Shilton
does these exercises. Maybe I'll never hear those people
at Wembley. Maybe his day'll be playing for Crewe
Alexandra the year they get to the third round of the Cup

and draw Liverpool, and get beat six–nil. Grandchildren,
meet the man who held the Reds to six when the Kop
wanted ten. I picked the ball out of the net four times for
Kenny Dalglish. Shake the hand which touched but
didn't quite save Phil Neal's penalty. Feel the shirt which
Ray Clemence swapped me at the end. That would be a
day. And what do *I* say, Mr McNab? That there's
thousands of Fords being scrapped every year
that I put three-and-a-half-minutes work on? Sorry,
I'll shut up now.

(**Keith Sanderson enters.**)

MCNAB Yes, Keith?

KEITH Mrs Adekunle's looking for you, sir.

MCNAB Good. Good.

KEITH Can you come, sir? I can't speak Nigerian.

MCNAB Tell her one minute. You've got enough Nigerian for
that, haven't you, Keith?

KEITH Oh yes, sir.

(**Exit Keith.**)

MCNAB Can I say what I would like to see happen? If Clive gets
signed, he'll have a couple of months before his CSEs. He
could get five, if you and I give him a good kick up
the rear. You see, Mr McNab, I don't think seventy to
thirty are very good odds.

MR POPE A good kick up the thingie. Right.

MCNAB And if they don't sign him . . .

MR POPE There's Coventry as well, and Arsenal.

MCNAB I mean, if nobody signs him. He'll need to be picked up
and faced with the need to get these qualifications. Get
the CSEs and then, who knows? 'O' levels perhaps. Good.

(**Keith Sanderson reappears.**)

MRS POPE Thank you, Mr McNab.

MCNAB   I'm coming, Keith. I'm coming. Well, goodbye.

(Keith sees what Mrs Pope has not, that Mr Pope has his radio ear-piece back in.)

KEITH   What's the score, Mister?

MR POPE   One all. Twenty minutes to go.

(Keith is pleased and follows Mr McNab out.)

MRS POPE   Have you listened to a single word he's said to you?

MR POPE   Yes.

MRS POPE   You haven't.

MR POPE   I have. He talked a lot of sense.

MRS POPE   I didn't notice he had time to say anything.

MR POPE   We could have killed ourselves on that bike, if Gene hadn't slowed down so we could touch his gloves.

MRS POPE   Christ. Come on. Back home!

MR POPE   Oh yeah. *(Checks watch.)* 'Sportsnight'.

(They go off.)

SCENE 5   **At the club: the Manager's office, where** IAN **is trying to get to grips with his new job. He is on the phone to the next office.**

IAN   Margaret, any more calls from the press about whether I'm applying for Gordon's job, the answer's yes. Any other questions, no comment.

(Ian puts the phone down. He gives himself a few seconds to savour being the manager. He sees that the team photograph is crooked. He straightens it. The phone rings.)

Dublin? What do they want? Yes, put them on. Ian Anderson here. Yes, I am the acting manager. Alan Boyd? Yes. Hold on please. *(Cups phone.)* Pete! Peter Miller! *(Back to phone)* I won't keep you a minute.

(PETE appears in a towel.)

Get Boydie in here quick.

PETE   Right. *(Goes off shouting.)* Alan Boyd. Boss's office. Alan Boyd.

IAN   And when is this match? Sunday week? Look you know this club will have to be safe from relegation by then or we won't be able to release him. He'll be even more choked if he's playing Third-Division football next season.

(FRANK FORD **enters after knocking.**)

(Into phone) Excuse me. What is it, Frank?

FRANK   I had an appointment with Gordon, me birthday's coming up.

IAN   Give me a couple of minutes, Frank.

(Frank nods and ALAN BOYD and Pete, both in towels, enter. There is a lot of noise from the corridor.)

IAN   Alan Boyd's with me now. I'll put him on.

BOYD   What's this about, Ian? They don't count after twelve.

IAN   *(Hands Boyd the phone.)* Pete, what's that racket?

BOYD   Alan Boyd.

PETE   They April-fooled one of the APs onto the street with no clothes on. It's all right, he's in now.

BOYD   Yes.

PETE   They had to let him in. There was two nuns passing the ground.

BOYD   You're the Irish FA. *(Cups phone.)* Ian, they don't count after lunchtime. *(Into phone)* You want me to play for Eire against Poland? Only one small problem with that – I'm not Irish.

IAN   *(Speaking into phone)* Can you hang on a minute? Boydie, it's not an April fool. They do want you. You've got an Irish grandfather. Gordon recommended you two seasons ago.

BOYD   *(Taking phone again)* Yes, this is Alan Boyd back again.

PETE   A first cap at twenty-nine. Jammy bleeder!

BOYD   'Course I want to. Yes. Yes. Yes. *(Puts phone down.)* Blimey, Republic of Ireland? I've never been there.

IAN   Boydie, you know what I'm going to say to you, don't you?

BOYD   What Ian?

IAN   That match in Warsaw is on Sunday week. If this club isn't mathematically safe by the end of the Wrexham game, you can't play for Eire. Sorry.

BOYD   Oh come on, Ian!!

IAN   What if you come back crocked? We play Newcastle the Tuesday after! Sorry, Boydie.

BOYD   Christ!

IAN   Look, Boydie, I played three years with you. I'm this side of the table now.

BOYD   Seven points out of three games? That's Warsaw out.

IAN   Boydie, go and get yourself a Polish phrase-book. Be positive.

BOYD   You think we can do it?

IAN   Yes I do. Go on, right away, and send in Frankie Ford for me will you, Pete?

PETE   Right.

(Boyd and Pete go out. After a few seconds, Frank enters.)

IAN   OK, Frankie. Come in, son. Come in, Frank. *(Into phone)* Margaret, get one of the APs to go out and get me a couple of cheese rolls, will you? I'm going to be here till midnight. You want anything, son?

FRANK   No thanks.

IAN   Two cheese rolls. And no more calls until I tell you. OK?

(Puts down phone and looks at Frank.)

IAN   Right. Eighteenth birthday in July, Frankie?

FRANK   The seventh.

IAN   Sorry son, we're not going to sign you professional. *(Pause)* You were expecting it, weren't you son?

FRANK   I don't know.

IAN   Now we said to you, we said to you when you first came here, that we thought you could make a living in this game, if you developed along the lines we hoped you would. If I was going to sign you, Frankie, I would want a keeper that I could play in the first team next season, if I had injuries to my two senior keepers. And in my judgement we couldn't do that. Your reflexes are good, you've got a fair pair of hands and you've worked bloody hard at your game, but your defenders never know a hundred per cent whether you're going to come and attack a cross or leave it to them. It's a fault you've tried to eliminate but . . . it's true, isn't it? Now, there are three possibilities from this situation. First, football. A lower grade of professional football. If you want us to try and find you another club . . . Brentford have rung us . . . might be able to fix you up with a month's trial down there. Second, work and football. Semi pro; your brother's at Ilford, isn't he? Well. Three, full-time work. Now, is there anything in that area that would interest you?

FRANK   I've done a bit of decorating with me uncle.

IAN   How did you get on with that?

FRANK   It was all right.

IAN   Or, of course, there's a trade. You'll be a couple of years behind, but we've got various contacts through our supporters.

FRANK   I shall have to . . .

IAN   You'll have to have a think. Talk it over with your Mum and Dad. Your brother.

FRANK   What division's Brentford in?

IAN   Fourth. Any problems telling your Dad?

FRANK   He won't believe it.

IAN   Want me to give him a call for you?

FRANK   No, I'll do it.

IAN   I'm glad you said that, Frankie. You've got character, son.

FRANK   Yeah.

IAN   You don't think we're right, do you Frank?

FRANK   What?

IAN   Our assessment of your play?

FRANK   No.

IAN   Good. Thirteen years ago Port Vale told me I was never going to be a player. Eighteen months later I was playing in the Second Division. I want you to say: 'What does that bloke know about goalkeeping? I'm going to come back here in a couple of years time with a First Division club, and I'm going to make that lot weep for letting me go.' Pop in any time. OK, Frank.

(Frank goes out. He passes Pete on his way in.)

PETE   Nice lad.

IAN   That's what I hate. Having to get rid of a guy who gives everything, and some of these monkeys you have to take never give you even ninety per cent. *(Pause)* I just want to go through this schools list with you. See if we agree on who we should offer apprentice forms to. Right?

PETE   Right.

IAN   Stephen Dean?

PETE   No. Coward. Both the wingers. One good clatter and you'll never see either of them again.

IAN   Byron Phillips?

PETE   No, he was marginal from the start.

IAN   Wayne Marshall?

PETE   Not for me.

IAN   Pity. He was so good when he was fourteen.

PETE His brother Kevin's going to be a smashing little player though.

IAN How old's he?

PETE Eleven. I've seen him a couple of times over the marshes Sunday morning.

IAN Micky Fielder?

PETE Definite for me. Here, you know his uncle's got some connection with Stoke City? Delivers their pies or something. He's trying to persuade Micky's Dad to get him in up there. I think we ought to clarify things there. Quick.

IAN Henry Holt? Got to have him.

PETE Oh yes. Get him shouting. Could have another Viv Anderson there. Get his aggression going. He's too nice.

IAN Clive Pope?

PETE I don't like short goalkeepers.

IAN His Dad's five foot ten and a half. He'll grow. He's got everything else. Agility. He's got good judgement.

PETE I know. I know.

IAN What's the problem?

PETE This young guy, Jerry Barclay. Fifteen. Five–eleven already. I've seen him in five district games this season, and he's good.

IAN If he's that good, we'll take him next year.

PETE Ian! Ian! If we take Clive next season and take Barclay the season after, what are we going to do with two youth keepers for one youth team the season after next?

IAN Hmmm.

PETE Look, I'd back my judgement on the boy Barclay. Play an amateur or a schools keeper next year. Clive, if he wants to . . .

IAN   His Dad wouldn't let him. He's set his heart on being signed pro. Besides Coventry City's supposed to be still looking at him.

PETE   He won't go to Coventry.

IAN   Why not?

PETE   He lives five minutes from the ground. If you want him, you can sign him. He's a homer. He don't go out.

IAN   But you'd wait for the boy Barclay?

(Pete nods.)

IAN   We'll see how Clive shapes on Saturday. I'd like to have him here. What's the schools picture like for next year?

PETE   The Dads are getting cagier. They don't want to sign anything. Competitive? If I went to a nursery schools match I'd run into the Spurs and West Ham scouts and Palace. Fulham? – most of their youth they got out of Dagenham. Don't nobody play in West London!

IAN   Nobody slipping through our system then, Pete?

PETE   Ian, I've seen every schools player in East London who can pass a ball accurately over five yards. But so has everybody else.

(Scene changes to the club dressing room. Frank Ford is sitting on the bench, head in hands. Boyd comes through singing 'When Irish eyes are smiling' from the shower.)

BOYD   All right, Frank?

FRANK   Yeah.

BOYD   Made use of my penalty tip yet?

FRANK   Not yet. Thanks though.

(Boyd looks at him and understands what's happened. He is going to say something, then doesn't. He goes off, still singing.)

FRANK   Bastards! Bastards!

(Blackout.)

SCENE 6   A week later: the Pope home as the parents prepare for Ian Anderson's visit. CLIVE is doing his stretching in the lounge. Both parents are off-stage.

MR POPE   Too late for that now, Clive.

MRS POPE   Clive, come and bring these biscuits through.

CLIVE   Ian don't eat between meals, Mum.

MR POPE   Coventry don't keep saying a good big un'll always beat a good little 'un, like this lot do; they're still interested.

MRS POPE   Are Coventry City a good club?

MR POPE   A very good club. Better than this lot. Was it his fault they lost six–one to Spurs?

MRS POPE   Not those, Clive, the best biscuits.

CLIVE   They thought I played all right against Spurs. It was you that didn't.

MR POPE   Biscuits!

MRS POPE   Coventry's too far away. Not that he's signing anything till he's revised for those exams.

MR POPE   We sign. He don't sign.

MRS POPE   We'd never see him. Does Ian prefer tea or coffee, Clive?

CLIVE   Tea, I think. I've seen the apprentices making him tea.

MRS POPE   Well, he can have either. We got both.

CLIVE   You don't think they want me at Coventry, do you?

MR POPE   I don't know one way or the other, but I do know if you'd had some support from those central defenders of yours it wouldn't have been six–one. Ian had to be at that one – he didn't come to the Watford one when you were excellent.

MRS POPE   Do they blame him for that then?

MR POPE   Stands to reason they do. I heard Pete shouting away. Clive, are you wearing a tie?

CLIVE   No.

MR POPE   Put your club tie on, son. They like the smart casual. I'm wearing a tie.

CLIVE   Maybe they'll sign you then.

MRS POPE   Clive!

MR POPE   Is that how your mate Walcott speaks to his father?

CLIVE   He hasn't got one.

MR POPE   Well you have.

MRS POPE   Alf! Would Coventry be better on the further education side?

MR POPE   I don't know. They all have to offer schemes. The FA makes 'em. And then there's the Arsenal situation.

CLIVE   Dad, there isn't an Arsenal situation. They weren't watching me at the Essex match. They were watching Walcott and that Hampshire number eight.

MR POPE   Arsenal watching Walcott? He isn't Irish. How many coloureds they got down Arsenal? They were watching you.

(The door bell rings.)

MR POPE   Clive, get your tie on. I'll go. If he says Clive's too short, know what, I'm never going to watch that club again. *(Goes to the door.)* Ian, come in!

(IAN ANDERSON **enters.**)

IAN   Mr Pope, Mrs Pope.

MRS POPE   Hello, Ian.

MR POPE   No news of the manager situation then, Ian?

IAN   Not yet.

MR POPE   You're on the short list though. It was in the paper.

IAN   You're a long way up here, aren't you?

MR POPE   Lift's not bust, is it Ian?

IAN   No.

MR POPE   Pity those centre-backs of Pete's didn't give Clive much protection against Spurs, Ian. Not that he complained. He's always been a good team player. Still, six–one wasn't bad against a youth team as strong as Spurs.

MRS POPE   A cup of coffee, Ian, or would you prefer tea? We've got both.

MR POPE   Clive's just putting his club tie on.

IAN   Tea would be good. Do you know, I can never get the APs to make me a good cup of tea down there. They just don't give the bag a good squeeze. Some of them don't even take the bag out of the cup.

MR POPE   You'll get a good cup of tea off Clive if you . . . you know.

(Clive comes down.)

IAN   Hello, son.

CLIVE   Hello, Ian.

(Ian makes himself comfortable and they wait for him to speak.)

IAN   Well, I'm not going to beat about the bush. We want to sign Clive as an apprentice professional.

(Long pause.)

MR POPE   Christ! Jesus Christ. I knew that Spurs result wouldn't cloud your judgement Ian.

IAN   Clive played a good game against Spurs.

MR POPE   I know. Hear that, Cath? Hear that, son? I mean obviously we've still got the Arsenal and Coventry City to consider. You're not worried about his height? Well, not with me being five foot ten. I knew you wouldn't be. Arsenal aren't.

MRS POPE   Thanks very much, Ian.

IAN   I didn't realise you had such a good view of the ground from here, Mr Pope. With a good pair of binoculars you could save yourself two pounds.

MR POPE   I don't want to save money, Ian. I stand on the terraces.

IAN   What is it, five minutes walk, Clive?

CLIVE   When the lift's working.

IAN   Very handy. That's the club I want to talk about. Not Coventry City. Not Arsenal. That club. I brought something to show you, Mr Pope. The club's cheque book. The one we use to sign players. Watch your hands, it's a bit dusty. That's the way the bank wants it. What does that mean to you and Clive? It means that if this club . . . no, not if . . . when this club makes an assault on the Second Division title in the next three seasons, we'll be doing it not with big money players, but with boys from this area who'll be getting their chance, some of them at sixteen and seventeen years of age. Eight of the side which kept us in the Second Division at Cambridge Saturday were under nineteen. That's what I'm offering. We're hoping Clive's going to grow. Five ten and a half, five eleven and built to match. Shilton, eh Clive? Character we've got no worries about. Home life . . . well we know that's going to be very conducive when he's away from us. If you work with the club, I think we'll produce a goalkeeper and a man to be proud of. That's all I want to say. If you want him to have a further education, Mrs Pope, you know all he's got to do is come and ask. His duties at the club, the money, well, Mr Pope probably knows more about that than I do. All I want you to do is to think of the day, possibly in eighteen months time, on that ground down there, when Clive'll come out of that tunnel into the light of the stadium in the first-team strip. A proud father and a proud mother in two good seats in the stand, guests of the club.

MR POPE   Hear that, Cath?

IAN   But there's a lot of hard work before that.

MR POPE   Right. Well, we've certainly got something to think about, haven't we? So, Ian, would you advise us to go and look round Coventry? It's for a week.

IAN   Certainly.

MRS POPE	Would you?
IAN	You want the best for your boy. I would do the same if I was in your position. I'd want to see everything.
MRS POPE	Bit far.
IAN	Perhaps.
MR POPE	Good then.
IAN	*(Rising to go)* It's a First Division club, and we can't offer that. Yet. Bye.

(Mr and Mrs Pope see him out. Clive stands in the middle of the room and salutes a non-existent crowd. Mr and Mrs Pope come back.)

MR POPE	I thought I was going to have a heart attack. Professional, son!
MRS POPE	He was very straight, I'll say that.
MR POPE	Next stop summer training, Clive! *(Goes and picks up Clive and carries him.)*
MR POPE	We are the champions. We are the champions. Champions.

SCENE 7 The club dressing room, during the first week of summer training. HENRY exhausted in training kit, sits slumped and breathing deeply.

(WALCOTT comes in. They do a tired version of their slap handshake. Walcott slumps down.)

HENRY	I thought I was fit.
WALCOTT	Don't talk to me brother. I'm dead.
HENRY	Ian says the real training starts next week.
WALCOTT	What's this then?
HENRY	Come on, we've got thirty pairs of boots to do.
WALCOTT	Give us a minute. I think I'm going to be sick.
HENRY	I'll be in the boot room.

(Henry goes off.)

WALCOTT   Tresor! Marius! They're killing me here. And they say they're giving us an easy week to start.

(CLIVE **enters, also exhausted.**)

CLIVE   Who you talking to, Walcott?

WALCOTT   God.

CLIVE   They said it was different training full-time. They were right. *(Pause)* What's your job?

WALCOTT   Boots.

CLIVE   Dressing rooms. *(Pause)* The first team don't talk to you, do they?

WALCOTT   No.

CLIVE   They're going to Ireland pre-season. *(Pause)* Have you got your cheque book?

WALCOTT   Yeah. It came to my landlady's this morning. Barclays Bank. I don't know what's wrong with cash.

CLIVE   Pete says it's supposed to be character-building.

WALCOTT   What's character-building about having a cheque book?

CLIVE   It's professional.

(Pause.)

WALCOTT   He don't like me.

CLIVE   Who?

WALCOTT   Ian

CLIVE   That's his way. You've got to be hard. That's why they kicked Gordon out. He was a gentleman.

WALCOTT   I should have gone to Charlton when they asked me.

CLIVE   Be the same at Charlton, wouldn't it?

WALCOTT   Did you see that run I did in the practice, that run out of defence? That was just like Tresor did against Italy in the World Cup. You never get any credit for doing right things. He's only looking for wrong things. Tackle back, close down. I go forward. That's my game. He don't want that.

CLIVE   You've got to tackle back.

WALCOTT   *(Indicating dunce's white bib)* Look, this is the third day I've been given this bloody thing. The worst trainer of the day. He's praising Micky Fielder, and I'm twice as good as Micky. Aren't I?

(IAN appears at the door.)

IAN   What's Henry doing the boots on his own for, Walcott Burns? This isn't a rest home. Go on. *(Pause)* You all right, Walcott?

(Walcott nods and goes.)

IAN   You can clean out the first-team dressing room now, Clive. Then in here, and then the ref's room.

CLIVE   What have we got tomorrow, Ian?

IAN   A little relaxing cross country. What position were you last time?

CLIVE   Fourth.

IAN   Not your strong event, is it?

CLIVE   *(As Ian goes off)* We'll see.

SCENE 8   The club dressing room, the first weeks of summer training.

(PETE comes in and starts putting out towels. He checks a stop-watch and puts more towels out. IAN enters.)

IAN   None of them back yet, Pete?

PETE   I only started 'em *(checking watch)* forty-seven minutes ago.

IAN   Seven miles or nine?

PETE   Seven, I don't want 'em dead before the start of the season.

IAN   Micky Fielder should be under fifty minutes. *(Going)* I'll be in the office. Give us a shout when they're all in and take down the finishing order, Pete, OK?

PETE   Ball work this afternoon?

IAN   Yes.

(He goes out.)

PETE   *(Checking watch again)* Come on, Micky Fielder, you tell me you're the new David Bedford, let's be having you.

(Enter ALAN BOYD. He is just back from the US and it's the first time anyone has seen him.)

PETE   Hello, Boydie. How did you get on over there? What was it, Minneapolis?

BOYD   Minnesota. The Minnesota Marauders. Where's the first team?

PETE   Ian sent them home. They've got a practice match against Dagenham tonight. Get on well?

BOYD   They want me back next summer.

PETE   I know where to come for a loan then. Come on, Micky Fielder!

BOYD   Have a good summer? You look like you had a couple too many paellas.

PETE   We never got there. Sitting in Gatwick for three days with the kids going mad. We said sod it, let's cut our losses and go home and paint the kitchen.

BOYD   *(Showing evening paper)* Ian seen this?

PETE   What?

BOYD   New manager. Eddie Quinn.

PETE   For here?

BOYD   Hasn't he said anything?

PETE   Nothing.

BOYD   He must have been told! He's on the short list.

(Enter MICKY FIELDER and CLIVE almost together. Clive just wins.)

PETE   Well done, Clive Pope! Well done, son! *(To Micky)* David Bedford? You are sure you didn't mean the Duke of

Bedford? What time do you call this? My wife could run that course in fifty minutes. *(Holding up dunce's bib)* Who's going to be last in?

(**The two boys crawl away to the seats to get a breather.**)

MICKY   It's hot out there, Pete!

PETE   Hot? Fifty-two minutes for that course? You're lucky I don't send you round again, Micky Fielder. Fourth place in the Inter-Counties? Who fixed the others? Or did your Dad meet you with his scooter at the first bend?

(HENRY HOLT **enters from run.**)

PETE   Fifty-three minutes. Well done, Henry. And where is Walcott Burns? He tackles like Dorothy Squires and now he can't even run no more. John Mitchell I don't expect for a couple of minutes. He's a central defender. You've got to compete in these cross countries or we won't get anything out of it! I want you two under fifty minutes Monday, right, or I'm letting my dog loose on you.

(**Enter** JOHN MITCHELL, **exhausted.**)

PETE   Well done, John Mitchell. Well done, son. That's a personal best: 53.35. You see what this boy's done here? He's competing.

(**Ian comes in and looks around.**)

IAN   Hello, Boydie. How did you get on over there? Where's Walcott Burns?

HENRY   He was just behind us in the forest.

IAN   Deep breathing, lads. Come on. Breath. You're regretting letting these bodies get out of condition, some of you, aren't you, and we start the real training tomorrow.

(**Ian sees the paper that Boyd has left on the seat and goes to leaf through it.**)

IAN   *(Looking at something on the back page)* Cloughie again, eh?

(Then he turns to the inside back page, which is what Boyd has been looking at. He reads the item. It is obvious that nothing has been said to him. Pause. WALCOTT comes in, exhausted. Ian checks his watch and then gets a white bib (the dunce's shirt) and throws it at Walcott.)

IAN Put it on, Walcott Burns! Fifty-four minutes for that course's a bloody disgrace! Either you can't run, in which case we can't use you, or you weren't trying, which is worse. Thirty press-ups.

WALCOTT I'm knackered.

IAN Thirty press-ups and then you might be knackered.

(Walcott sinks down and starts doing the press-ups, not very well.)

IAN Fifty-four minutes. John Mitchell's in front of you. It's a joke, son. Start again from the beginning and this time keep your knees straight. If you don't want to play for this club, which requires you to be fit, bloody fit, then you can get lost now and stop wasting our time. We're not an amateur football club. Get those arms locked out unless you want to start again. That's seven.

WALCOTT That's nine.

IAN You've done seven. And this afternoon I don't want any of that crap Danny La Rue tackling we had out of you yesterday. How many tackles did you make in that practice? I'll put it another way: how many times did you come away with the ball? How many?

WALCOTT None?

IAN How many?

WALCOTT None.

IAN Down lower. Get your chin on the floor. Like it is on match days. You'll win tackles this afternoon. *(To the rest)* Right, get some lunch for yourselves from the shop and we'll start again at two.

(Exit Ian, followed by Pete. They watch at the door as Walcott finishes his press-ups. He collapses. Ian comes back.)

IAN	Five more! And lock your arms out this time. Quickly.

(Walcott does five more press-ups at speed. Defiantly. He looks up at Ian, still in the up position. Ian turns on his heel and goes, muttering 'git', Walcott collapses.)

WALCOTT   I'll murder that bastard.

(He gets up and walks to a seat and collapses.)

BOYD   Who's the gaffer here?

JOHN   I am.

BOYD   John Mitchell, have these lads been initiated yet?

CLIVE   Eh?

JOHN   No.

BOYD   It's about time.

MICKY   What's this, Boydie?

BOYD   That's for the pros to know and you to find out.

MICKY   We are professional.

BOYD   Not until you've had the potion. Get the potion, John Mitchell.

(John and Henry go out.)

WALCOTT   What's going on?

BOYD   Starting with the race-winner, I think.

(Clive leaps up as John comes back with a plastic bucket of boot blacking.)

WALCOTT   Oh not that. It never comes off.

BOYD   Speaking from experience, I see. Right Henry, Micky, get him.

(A chase begins with Clive dodging in and out of the benches. He is finally caught. Henry and Micky hold him while the others take his clothes off. Clive struggles and swears. They set about the blacking.)

BOYD   I knew a trainer who used to tie a piece of string round their knackers and lead them round the corridors. One chap tried to run away with the string still round him. I believe he's singing with the Nolan sisters now.

(They finish. Clive is covered in blacking. They move away, leaving him.)

BOYD   Now you're a professional footballer.

(They all leave Clive alone.)

CLIVE   This'll go all over the sheets. My Mum'll murder me.

ACT TWO

SCENE 1   At the club: the manager's office, later that season. Lunch time: EDDIE QUINN, **the new manager, is on the phone. There are sandwiches in a tin on the desk.**

EDDIE   Yes. Yes. *(Cupping phone)* Ian! Ian! *(Into phone)* Can you hold on a minute, Mr Barclay, I'm going to ask my assistant manager to come round and see you. OK?

(IAN **enters.**)

EDDIE   Free Monday night?

IAN   Yes.

EDDIE   *(Back to the phone)* Monday night at seven thirty. Right, thanks, Mr Barclay. *(Puts down the phone.)* Crystal Palace have been round that boy's house! Why haven't we signed the boy on associated schoolboy forms, Ian?

IAN   The father wouldn't sign.

EDDIE   What's he like? Is he waiting for some club to drop a couple of grand in used notes on the kitchen table to help him make up his mind?

IAN   I don't know.

EDDIE   Well you should know. Sod letting Palace get a boy who lives five hundred yards from this ground. Sod that!

IAN   I'll talk to him.

EDDIE   Do you know Barclay's probably going to get an England trial? Right, if he gets one he'll turn up there in one of our tracksuits and a new pair of boots compliments of the club. Have you got his size?

IAN   Twelves.

EDDIE   Twelves on a fifteen-year-old. That's the size a goalkeeper should be. I want you to pick him for the youth team before Christmas.

IAN   Eddie, I can't just play him in the youth team. Clive's not injured.

EDDIE   Barclay's too good to mess around.

IAN   I've got an apprentice goalkeeper.

EDDIE   You've got a midget.

IAN   He's good and he's growing.

EDDIE   A quarter of an inch in the four months I've been here.

IAN   Nearly half an inch. He's working hard for us. He's agile . . .

EDDIE   Look Ian, I'm not arguing with you. Play Jerry Barclay. All right?

IAN   *(Pause)* OK.

EDDIE   I'm not talking about every game. I want him played every three or four games. I want him travelling to every match. I want Jerry Barclay going to bed in our strip, he's so proud of it. And that's another thing. That schools session you and Pete were taking Tuesday. I didn't want to call you out then, but those two new lads, Paul and that ginger one, both with other clubs' shirts. I'm not having that at this club. We've got plenty of strip they can use.

IAN   They were birthday presents probably.

EDDIE   I couldn't give a toss. If they want to wear Spurs kit let them go to White Hart Lane. If they speak Spanish they might get in. No school kit, no Spurs kit, no West Ham kit: our kit. Have a sandwich.

IAN   Right.

EDDIE   I want every car in this borough with one of our stickers
         in the back; I want the team picture up in every chip
         shop. I don't want to look out of the window and see kids
         in the street chalking up 'West Ham' on our walls. Sod
         West Ham, sod Spurs; this club's going up. And I want
         you to sell that to the parents of these kids. And I'll tell
         you this, Ian – if that first team doesn't start performing
         for me, I am putting your kids in. The two I had in the
         reserves Wednesday: Micky Fielder ran himself into the
         ground, and that Walcott Burns played a bloody good
         first half. Got a sense of space, that kid.

IAN   Yeah.

EDDIE   Don't you rate him?

IAN   He's good but he's flashy and he doesn't work.

EDDIE   He finds that vacant space, and you pay money for that.
         Keep at him.

         (ALAN BOYD **walks in.**)

IAN   Hello, Boydie.

EDDIE   Alan Boyd, you might be an international football player
         now but you've got something on the end of your arm,
         haven't you? Well, use it to knock on that door before
         you walk in. *(Boyd does so.)* Come in, Boydie, and tell us
         all about gay Paree.

BOYD   Gay Paree? Plane, hotel, training ground, hotel, match,
         hotel, plane home. I did see Notre Whatsit from me
         bedroom window last night.

IAN   Good result, getting a draw against France.

BOYD   Yeah. Can I get some training in with your boys this
         afternoon, Ian?

IAN   Of course you can.

EDDIE   Hear that? If I had eleven in the first team like him . . .
         Boydie, do the club a charity function Sunday.

BOYD   Oh Boss, ask Barry.

EDDIE   Barry always does it. They asked for you.

BOYD   What is it?

EDDIE   Some people collected a lot of money for buying the mongol kiddies a Transit. They want you to hand over the cheque. And take some photos. Come in tomorrow and I'll give you the details and you can take a cheque from us. Here, and ask the players for a whip round.

BOYD   Boss, I don't know what to say at those things.

EDDIE   Boydie, this is part of your job. Come on, you've just played in Paris, son. What have those little kiddies got? Go on, piss off. Well played, son. *(As Boyd goes off)* Right, Ian, let's look at our future.

SCENE 2   At the club: the apprentice dressing room; the same day. (WALCOTT **walks in eating some lunch out of a paper bag. There are some newspapers on the seats. Walcott picks one up and starts reading.** HENRY **comes in and also picks up a newspaper. On his way out, he passes** CLIVE.)

HENRY   I've stopped growing this month.

CLIVE   I nearly have 'an all. It doesn't matter for you, does it?

HENRY   They say it does.

           (Exit Henry.)

CLIVE   *(Looking at newspaper)* How does Pat Jennings get hands like he's got?

WALCOTT   His Mum pegged him up on the clothes-line when he was small to stretch him. It was in *Shoot*.

CLIVE   Leave it out. *(Takes out a letter.)* Here, look at this.

WALCOTT   Who's this? Carol?

CLIVE   Look at the address.

WALCOTT   You dirty . . .

CLIVE   I ain't.

WALCOTT   Portsmouth. This the one you met at the Portsmouth game?

CLIVE	Yeah.
WALCOTT	Well, well.
CLIVE	Ian gave us some stick. Look at the envelope.
WALCOTT	'To the small, dark goalkeeper. Youth team.'
CLIVE	She didn't even ask my name.
WALCOTT	'Dear small, dark goalkeeper, I long for the touch . . .'
CLIVE	It don't say that. Give it here. I don't want you to read it.
WALCOTT	For the touch of your 'Dino Zoff' gloves round my . . .
CLIVE	*(Snatching it back)* It's private.
WALCOTT	That's nice.
CLIVE	The only girl I met and she's got to live in Portsmouth.
WALCOTT	Did she come up to you?
CLIVE	Yes, she wanted my autograph.
WALCOTT	Well she should know your name then.
CLIVE	I don't do my signature so you can read it.
WALCOTT	Oh?
CLIVE	Says she might be coming up to London in the spring.
WALCOTT	Go down and see her. Get hold of a car and go down.
CLIVE	I ain't passed my test.
WALCOTT	So what? What's her name?
CLIVE	Carol.
WALCOTT	You want to get her to send you a picture.
CLIVE	I will. *(Pause)* Ian's got the needle into you again, hasn't he?
WALCOTT	Don't talk to me about that bastard . . .
CLIVE	*(Turning to door)* Hello, Ian!
WALCOTT	*(Realising it's a trick)* Get lost!

(MICKY FIELDER **comes in.**)

MICKY　Anyone lend us 50p till pay?

WALCOTT　Sorry, Mick, pictures skint me last night.

CLIVE　Sorry. I don't bring any except me dinner money. Here *(to both of them)* what was it like at Arsenal?

MICKY　Good.

WALCOTT　Yes, held 'em to four-one.

CLIVE　Who were you marking?

WALCOTT　Brian McDermott.

CLIVE　He's been on 'Match of the Day'.

MICKY　Talbot was playing an' all. Getting over his injury.

WALCOTT　It was great.

MICKY　Marble dressing rooms.

WALCOTT　They was tile. The entrance was marble.

MICKY　Oh yes, clean though, in' it? And that pitch.

WALCOTT　McDermott didn't score. Yes, when I walk out there and there ain't twenty people watching there's fifty grand and twenty. And they all boo like they did Norman Hunter. 'Burns, you black bastard!' And I'll give 'em a little bow and rip 'em apart. Jennings begs me to go easy after my first six 'cause his mother's watching.

(JOHN MITCHELL **enters, eating.**)

JOHN　Ian's got it in for you again then?

WALCOTT　Aghh!!

MICKY　Don't he like coloureds?

JOHN　He got on with . . . what's name . . .

MICKY　Oh yeah, Steven. Steven Osambale. Loved him.

JOHN　He just don't like Walcott!

WALCOTT　He's jealous.

JOHN	Played for Leicester City and he's jealous of you, you flash sod!!
MICKY	*(Looking at newspaper crossword)* There, are, 'expert at folding woollies'.
CLIVE	How many letters?
MICKY	Eight.

(Henry comes in again.)

JOHN	*(Taking up newspaper)* 'Expert at folding woollies', Henry? Eight letters.
HENRY	My mother, that's eight.
JOHN	Yeah, and it's two words an' all.
WALCOTT	*(With another newspaper)* Look at that.
HENRY	What?
WALCOTT	Tessa Sanderson.
HENRY	Cor.
WALCOTT	I'll cut that out and put it on my wall.
JOHN	You'll go blind.
WALCOTT	What a javelin-thrower. My old event.
JOHN	I could throw her something.
WALCOTT	What? What could you throw my Tessa, you dirty dog?
JOHN	Eh Clive?
WALCOTT	Don't bring him into it. He's lost his heart down Pompey way. 'Oh Carol, I was just a fool' . . .
JOHN	That? That one by the coach? I thought that was a bloke.
CLIVE	Shut up.
JOHN	Straight up. No, sorry Clive. It was a genuine mistake. Straight up, I thought it was a bloke.
CLIVE	In lipstick and a skirt?
JOHN	*(Winks to others)* Portsmouth, Clive.

WALCOTT   Leave him alone.

(PETE **comes in.**)

JOHN   Pete, 'expert at folding woollies'. Eight letters.

PETE   I shall have to give that some thought, son.

CLIVE   Pete, have you asked Eddie about what I asked you?

PETE   You've got a mouth, haven't you?

CLIVE   I thought you was going to have a word.

WALCOTT   What's this?

PETE   Not me, son. I've got my pension to think of.

JOHN   You won't get a pension from here, Pete.

PETE   I know, but I can still think about it.

(Pete is putting up the team for Saturday.)

CLIVE   Ain't Micky and Walcott playing for the reserves again, Pete?

PETE   No, Tony and Gregg are fit. *(To Walcott)* You're back with the good side now.

CLIVE   What are we doing this afternoon, Pete?

PETE   Ball work. We only do ball work here. Right, what's everybody getting me for Christmas?

JOHN   What do you want, Pete?

PETE   Only one thing I want, son, and you couldn't get it for me.

JOHN   What's that?

PETE   A new pair of knees so I could play football again.

CLIVE   Is that what goes, Pete?

PETE   Yep, you've still got your skill, you've still got your vision, if you ever had any, John Mitchell, but if you ain't got your knees you can't get there. You ain't got a game. Look at Di Stephano.

JOHN   Who?

PETE	Wonderful player but without the speed . . . gone.
WALCOTT	You can have mine, Pete.
PETE	Yeah, I'd look a right idiot with white thighs and black knees. Look like a draughts board.
WALCOTT	A hundred thousand.
PETE	Done. That'll be half my wages. Still. You don't know you're born, you lot. You can go out there for ninety minutes and play a beautiful game. You can play football. I have to watch you.
CLIVE	Pete, you going to talk to Eddie about the ref's room?
WALCOTT	What's this about?
CLIVE	Well, you know me and him have to clean the dressing rooms and the ref's room . . .
MICKY	We were here till nearly five o'clock last night.
PETE	You don't know you're born, you lot.
CLIVE	We can't clean the ref's room – it'd only take us a couple of minutes – because Eddie don't change after training. He goes straight in and does his office work in his track-suit.
MICKY	So we can't clean, see, and we've finished the other jobs at quarter past three.
CLIVE	We could come in five minutes early next morning.
WALCOTT	Well, ask him then!
JOHN	Grow up!
CLIVE	Henry, he likes you.

(Henry shakes his head.)

WALCOTT	Go and ask him, Clive. It's reasonable.
JOHN	Grow up!
WALCOTT	He can only say no.
CLIVE	Oh yeah.

JOHN   You'd go if it was your job, I suppose?

WALCOTT   Yeah.

PETE   Don't know you're born.

JOHN   Well, go on then.

WALCOTT   I'm on boots.

JOHN   You're all mouth, Walcott. Tresor?! Don't make me laugh.

(**Walcott gets up and goes.**)

CLIVE   Christ!

JOHN   He's gone into the bog for ten minutes. Then he'll come back and tell us he's been in to Eddie.

(**Henry gets up and goes out in the same direction as Walcott. He comes back.**)

HENRY   No, he hasn't.

JOHN   Well, somewhere else then.

PETE   You don't know you're born, you lot. What do you do? Clean a few boots, a bit of sweeping, taking the first-team kit out, you're off in the middle of the afternoon most days. Twenty-five pounds a week? Money for old rope.

JOHN   Different in your day, Pete?

PETE   Bloody was, you cheeky monkey. Ground staff, son, not apprentices. Now that was work. Cutting grass, sweeping up terraces, painting the stands, cleaning cars, running errands, doing the post, for a couple of shillings a week. You never saw a ball. They didn't believe in it.

JOHN   Why not?

PETE   They wanted you starved of it. They wanted you to slaver at the mouth at the sight of a ball on Saturday. Every one of you got your own ball for your individual skills. You don't know you're born. He won't get any change out of the manager with that request.

JOHN   He hasn't gone.

MICKY	Why didn't you stop him then, Pete?
PETE	What do you learn by, Micky Fielder?
MICKY	Mistakes.
PETE	That's right, son.

**(Scene changes to the manager's office.
EDDIE and IAN are going over the youth-team staff. Walcott knocks.)**

EDDIE	Come in.

(Walcott enters.)

Yes, Walcott?

WALCOTT	It's all right if you're busy, sir.
EDDIE	What is it?
WALCOTT	I'll leave it.
EDDIE	What's on your mind, Walcott?
WALCOTT	Well, you know . . . well, when you come in . . . you know after training. I could come back when . . .
EDDIE	I come back after training? Yes.
WALCOTT	Yeah. And two APs have to do the ref's room . . . you know, where you change.
EDDIE	Yes.
WALCOTT	Well, sir, they can't sweep it till you're changed. Well, the thing is they've finished the other jobs quite a bit before that. And they have to wait around. So what they thought . . .
EDDIE	Yes, what did they think?
WALCOTT	Well, could you change before you did your phoning and that? That'd make it easier for them, and they could get away.
EDDIE	*(After pause)* You wouldn't like me to change in the street? *(Pause as Walcott's discomfort is savoured)* No, I'm trying to find some way of fitting into your arrangements, Walcott. Maybe I shouldn't bother to come in at all, if I get in the apprentices' way.

WALCOTT   Well, it's not . . .

EDDIE   You may be too dozy to notice, Walcott, but I'm trying to run a football club here. Anything else?

(Walcott shakes head and goes.)

IAN   See what I mean – flash?

EDDIE   Yeah, but he's got bottle. Good, we can use that. You've got a training session, haven't you?

(Ian goes. The scene changes back to the dressing room.)

PETE   When you taking your test, Clive Pope?

CLIVE   They put me in for it, but you have to wait months.

(ALAN BOYD **enters in his training kit. He is respectfully acknowledged.)**

PETE   Good result in Paris, Boydie.

BOYD   *(Taking out French international shirt)* Where's Walcott?

HENRY   Cor!

PETE   He's discussing something with the manager.

HENRY   Is that Tresor's shirt?

BOYD   No, I wasn't near him at the end. Lopez, this was.

HENRY   *(Disappointed)* Ah.

JOHN   Great, Boydie.

PETE   Just saying, this generation, Boydie, don't know they're born. Taking car tests.

BOYD   Who?

CLIVE   Me.

BOYD   How's your emergency stop?

PETE   With a goalkeeper's reactions he should be sending the tester through the windscreen. You'd better tell him you're a keeper, Clive. Make sure he's wearing his seat belt.

BOYD   When I had my first test for a moped, the tester says, after a bit, 'Right, Mr Boyd, I'm going to go off down this street now and I want you to circle this block, and at some point I'm going to jump out in front of you and, of course, I shall want you to stop right away.' So I started going, round and round for twenty minutes, twenty minutes and no sign of this tester. So anyway, I went back to the testing place to see what had happened.

CLIVE   What had, Boydie?

BOYD   It turned out my tester had jumped out in front of another moped that wasn't even doing the test. Multiple fractures.

(They laugh as Walcott comes in.)

PETE   Manager see it your way, Walcott?

(Walcott goes to his place as Henry holds up the shirt.)

HENRY   Look at this.

WALCOTT   Hey!

HENRY   It's not Tresor's. He wasn't at that end, were you, Boydie?

WALCOTT   What was he like, Boydie? Did you touch him?

(Ian enters.)

IAN   Right . . . hello, Boydie . . . right, get the kit in the van. We're going to the park.

JOHN   Ian, 'expert at folding woollies'?

IAN   Come on, lads. And you, Walcott. How many letters?

JOHN   Eight.

IAN   Eight? Get a move on.

JOHN   Yeah.

IAN   'Expert at folding woollies'. Eight.

(All go out, except John, who has left his paper with Ian.)

IAN   Shepherd.

(Blackout.)

SCENE 3   On the park. (PETE MILLER and CLIVE enter. They start Clive's goalkeeping warm-ups. ALAN BOYD follows and starts his own individual warm-up. IAN leads on MICKY, HENRY, WALCOTT and JOHN.)

IAN   Right! When the opposition has the ball in our half of the field, our midfield players are defenders. Right? And they'll defend as if they mean it. They go in where it hurts, or they get out of it. Right. First group. Henry Holt defending. Opposing wideman – John Mitchell. Micky Fielder. Nip in and nick it, Micky.

(They start exercise. Micky nicks the ball.)

PETE   That's it. See, Walcott?

(They repeat the exercise and Micky nicks the ball.)

IAN   Right, that's what we want on Saturday. Next group. Opposing wideman – Alan Boyd. Pete Miller defending. Walcott Burns!

(Boyd skilfully draws the ball away from Walcott and attacks Pete.)

PETE   Come on, Walcott. Tackle!

(Walcott misses tackle.)

IAN   AGAIN!!

(Second try just as bad.)

IAN   Christ!

PETE   Tackle!

(The next sequence should happen in slow motion. Boyd moves to the ball, with Walcott close behind. Boyd slowly feints; Walcott is lunging with his foot. He hits Boyd just above the ankle. Boyd falls against Pete Miller. Very slowly they both fall to the ground, as Boyd starts to clutch his leg.)

PETE   You're supposed to kick the ball, not kick him!

BOYD   *(Clutching knee)* Christ!!!

PETE   What is it, Boydie?

(Pete goes to grab him up.)

BOYD   Don't!!

PETE   Ian!

IAN   John Mitchell, get to the phone – reverse charges to the club, make sure the physio's there. We're going back. Back in the van. Go!

(**The apprentices, except Walcott, leave.**)

PETE   It's not broken.

WALCOTT   I went for the ball.

BOYD   My bastard knee!!

IAN   *(Lifting from the shoulder)* Keep your other leg against it, Boydie. That stupid idiot!!

(**They slowly take Boyd off.**)

SCENE 4   At the club. PETE and EDDIE, **wearing an overcoat, are in the dressing room.**

EDDIE   So it was an ordinary training session?

PETE   Yes.

EDDIE   Just an ordinary training session, nicking the ball off an attacker when your defender is holding him off?

PETE   Yes.

EDDIE   Have you sent everyone home?

PETE   Yes.

EDDIE   No special tension, no . . . *(Pause)*

PETE   No.

EDDIE   Ian thinks it was deliberate.

PETE   What?

EDDIE   How did you see it?

PETE   Me? Have you asked Boydie?

EDDIE   He's in hospital with twisted ligaments. The earliest he's going to be back is February. I'm not going to him for an objective opinion, am I? Now, how did you see it?

PETE   Well . . .

EDDIE   Pete, I've lost a vital player for the Christmas matches . . . there's no chance . . . now, they tell me . . . nothing like enough money to go into the market for a replacement so I'm not happy. I want to know whether we're encouraging a bloody maniac in the youth team over Christmas.

PETE   Deliberate? Walcott's not a dirty player. He's not even a hard player. That's been his trouble. We've been trying to motivate him on that part of his game. He ain't the best tackler we've got. Maybe that was it.

EDDIE   The one player we're relying on over Christmas, really relying on. And some half-baked AP has to clatter him into hospital. You'd think we had enough problems. *(Pause)* OK, Pete.

(Eddie makes to go.)

PETE   Merry Christmas, Boss.

EDDIE   Eh? Oh yeah. What you buying me, Pete? I'll take Diego Maradona in a Christmas cracker. Oh, and Pete . . .

PETE   Yeah?

EDDIE   Don't let Walcott Burns near me for the next couple of days. I'm damned if I'm going to get a coronary over him.

(Blackout.)

SCENE 5   **Christmas at the Pope home. (The** POPES **come through with their Christmas hats on.** WALCOTT **is with them but without a funny hat.)**

MR POPE   Right, what's on the box?

MRS POPE   Let it cool down. It's been on since ten o'clock.

MR POPE   For *Jailhouse Rock*, Cath! What did you think of him, Walcott? The King?

WALCOTT   He's all right.

MR POPE   All right? The King? All right? Beats that rubbish you kids have to put up with.

MRS POPE	Who wants a drink? Here, don't get settled. I'm not doing the cooking *and* the washing up.
MR POPE	I'll do it.
MRS POPE	*(With drink)* Walcott?
MR POPE	Now you got a choice here, Walcott, for your nip.
MRS POPE	Don't go mad with it.
MR POPE	I'm not going mad with it. Do you think I want Ian coming round here and telling me I've got his players drunk? This ain't Chelsea FC, is it, Walcott? Here Cath, what's this doing here?
MRS POPE	It's always on the tray. We're not drinking it.
MR POPE	Too bloody right we're not. Know what that is, Walcott? A bottle of 1937 Champagne, there y'are: 'Champagne de . . .' Well, you can read it. Know anything about champagne, Walcott?
WALCOTT	No.
MR POPE	Well, that's one of the top firms. Present from his uncle to be popped when Clive gets signed full pro.
CLIVE	In 2001.
MR POPE	Now pack that in. Where's your confidence? You're invited to that day, Walcott. It might be the same day they sign you. It'll be delicious.
MRS POPE	You can't hold champagne down. Remember your bass guitarist's wedding?
MR POPE	It'll be delicious on that day. Clive with Eddie Quinn, or whoever's there then, both looking at the camera, fountain pen poised over the professional forms. Me and Cath standing behind. Ian here. And Pete. No, not Pete, he'll be standing out of picture with that Jerry Barclay he thinks so much of. 'Champagne all round! Now what can we offer our guest? Sherry? I should pass on the sherry, Walcott, it's been there since last Christmas. Whiskey? Lager? And in your honour, Walcott, rum.

WALCOTT   Eh?

MR POPE   Rum. Well, it's your staple drink over there, ain't it?

WALCOTT   Over where? I was born in Hackney.

MR POPE   Yeah. But you've still got a bit of feeling for that old island in the sun, haven't you? 'Oh island in the sun . . .'

MRS POPE   Thank you.

WALCOTT   Thanks. I'll try that.

MR POPE   Just a tot, Cath. He's playing tomorrow.

WALCOTT   I'm not playing.

MR POPE   What's the matter? They changed the team? It was in the paper you was playing.

CLIVE   He's playing.

WALCOTT   I'm not.

MR POPE   Not been picked?

WALCOTT   I've been picked, but I'm not playing. I'm packing it in.

CLIVE   Not again.

MR POPE   I'm not listening to rubbish like that. Not playing! Cath, where's my snorkel? I'm going to do the washing up.

MRS POPE   Well, you don't have to make a meal of it.

MR POPE   And they're giving you games in the reserves? Act your age, Walcott! I'd be over the moon if Clive was getting games in the reserves. He's doing all right but he ain't got a game in the reserves yet. I never heard anything so stupid in my life. I'll come back when people are talking sense. Kids!

(**He goes out.**)

CLIVE   You're playing.

WALCOTT   I'm not playing.

MRS POPE   Have you told 'em?

CLIVE   He's playing.

WALCOTT   I'm not. They think I'm rubbish. Right, I'll be rubbish. I'm packing it in.

CLIVE   If they thought you were rubbish they wouldn't be playing you in the reserves tomorrow, would they?

WALCOTT   Ian thinks I'm rubbish.

CLIVE   He might say you're rubbish sometimes. That's to motivate you.

WALCOTT   That's supposed to motivate me? It's a waste of time. 'Think', they keep saying. 'Think!' They don't want you to think, they just want you to think what they're thinking.

CLIVE   'Course they do. What are you going to have, eleven men all playing different tactics?

WALCOTT   I'm not talking about tactics. They want yes-men.

(Mr Pope enters.)

MR POPE   You talked any sense into him yet, Clive?

CLIVE   No.

MR POPE   What are you going to do if you don't play football, Walcott?

WALCOTT   I'll be all right.

MRS POPE   He says nobody thinks he's no good.

MR POPE   He's in the reserves at just under seventeen 'cause he's no good? Hold me up.

WALCOTT   I think I'd better go. Thanks for the dinner and that.

MRS POPE   Where are you going?

WALCOTT   Back to my digs.

MRS POPE   Well, I'll tell you what you're going to do, Walcott, if you're not going to turn up tomorrow. You write 'em a note and drop it in to the ground. It's for your own benefit.

(Mr Pope goes off.)

WALCOTT   I don't have to write a note.

MRS POPE   You do.

WALCOTT   I haven't got a pen.

MRS POPE   *(Going)* I have.

CLIVE   Tell 'em you're ill.

WALCOTT   I'm not going to tell 'em I'm ill.

CLIVE   You're the most big-headed bastard I've ever met.

WALCOTT   Eh?

CLIVE   Do you know why they don't tell you you had a good game that much? Because you're big-headed enough already. They want to cut you down to size.

MRS POPE   *(Coming back)* There you are, Walcott.

CLIVE   *(After pause as Walcott looks at paper)* What you going to say?

WALCOTT   *(Pause)* I don't know. *(Longer pause)* I can't write it down. Christ.

MRS POPE   Walcott? Don't you enjoy playing?

WALCOTT   No. Just little bits, when I can't hear Ian shouting.

CLIVE   We're not payed to enjoy it, are we? We do. I do. *(Pause)* Why don't you go and take it out on Millwall reserves?

WALCOTT   I ain't got anything against Millwall reserves, have I?

CLIVE   You should have.

WALCOTT   Well I haven't. I can't write this.

MRS POPE   Well, you're going to have to play then, aren't you, and tell 'em you want to pack it in after.

(Blackout.)

SCENE 6   At the club. EDDIE is at his desk in the manager's office. (IAN comes in.)

EDDIE   *(Handing him three sheets)* That's our teams for Saturday. Pin 'em up, will you?

(**Ian looks at the third sheet.**)

IAN   I didn't pick Jerry Barclay.

EDDIE   He's playing.

IAN   But that's two games in a row. I told Clive Pope the odd game to give the Barclay boy a taste of the game at that level. This'll destroy him.

EDDIE   Don't talk nonsense, Ian. If that's going to destroy him it don't say a lot for his character, which you say he's got.

IAN   He's playing well. He's training well.

EDDIE   But he's stopped growing.

IAN   His mother and father are coming on the coach to Watford Saturday.

EDDIE   Clive'll travel. He's going to have to fight for his place like everybody else does here.

IAN   Do I pick the youth team?

EDDIE   That's not just the players, that's you, and that's me. Walcott Burns!

IAN   Yes.

EDDIE   He's playing like a zombie.

IAN   Yes.

EDDIE   Why?

IAN   He doesn't concentrate. He's all over the place.

EDDIE   Is it still that bloody tackle?

IAN   That's forgotten as far as I'm concerned.

EDDIE   Good. I wondered if it was. But has he forgotten it?

IAN   He'll have to. I'm not making any special concessions for him.

EDDIE   Send him in, Ian.

(**Ian goes, sending in** WALCOTT.)

EDDIE   Sit down, Walcott. Right, I think it's time for a cards-on-the-table situation.

WALCOTT   Well, I . . .

EDDIE   You'll get your turn, son. Motivation, Walcott. Motivation. *(He gets up and walks to the window.)* There's a lot of unfortunate people in this world, Walcott. Do you know that?

WALCOTT   Yeah?

EDDIE   Do you know what I was doing Sunday? *(Walcott shakes his head.)* You can see it from here. There's a school for spastic kiddies. They wanted us to come down and give out the prizes. When we got down there it turned out what they really wanted was for us to give them a game. Eleven youngsters in steel chairs against our first team. They asked me to play centre half for the cripples to even it up. So that was my problem sorted out for the afternoon – how to stop our first team getting a goal. Because I knew that that first team of mine don't like losing – not even to a team of cripples. Christ knows how we did it, ten minutes each way it was, but with a minute to go we were holding them nil–nil. I got 'em organised – blocking them out with their chairs, closing them down by ramming 'em with the wheels. We played like Italians. Then, in the last minute, Brownie breaks through. I'm covering the keeper; I'm covering this side of the goal. And Brownie lets a screamer go and it goes straight through my legs. Sod it, one–nil, I thought. And then there's this clatter behind me: steel, alloy or whatever they make those things of. And I look round and this chair's on the deck and this kid, this goalkeeper's two yards out of his chair but the ball's in his hands. Totally winded but the ball's in his hands. That's motivation! That's commitment! And that's what I'm not getting from you, Walcott. Sometimes it's there and sometimes it isn't. That's what I want to see you about. *(Pause)* Brownie followed up on that ball. I think he was going to kick the ball out of that kid's hands. Well, no one does that to my goalkeeper. I elbowed him out of the way. He was shouting some nonsense about professional foul all the way back in the car. Stephen Brown hasn't got your ability, but your ability isn't worth a light without what he's got. You just don't want to play.

WALCOTT   But I do want to play, sir.

EDDIE   You don't son. You don't.

WALCOTT   I do. But he doesn't like my play. He doesn't think I've got ability.

EDDIE   You think Ian's pressured you?

WALCOTT   Yes, sir.

EDDIE   Pressure? You haven't had pressure yet, Walcott. Your opponent's are going to pressure you twice as much as Ian's ever done.

WALCOTT   I'm getting better.

EDDIE   You're not. And you won't get better because you think you know it all. You don't think Ian's got anything to teach you, do you? Did you ever see him play for this club? Three or four years ago?

(Walcott shakes his head.)

I did.

WALCOTT   I want to play.

EDDIE   You want to work?

WALCOTT   Yes, sir.

EDDIE   You want to be a professional footballer?

WALCOTT   Yes, sir.

EDDIE   This had better be it, Walcott, because I haven't got time for all this. This isn't a nursery school. You make a decision and that's it as far as I'm concerned. You work with Ian; you work on what he thinks you need to work on. No aggravation, no muttering under your breath. You do it!!

WALCOTT   *(Nods)* Sir.

EDDIE   Right, you'll sub for the reserves Saturday.

WALCOTT   Great!

EDDIE   I'm going to take a lot of convincing, Walcott.

WALCOTT   Yes, sir.

EDDIE   On your way. Tresor!

            (Exit Walcott, happy.)

SCENE 7 **The club dressing room. IAN is putting the team notice up. PETE and ALAN BOYD are sitting on the benches.**

IAN   Are you going to stay and see the game, Boydie?

BOYD   No. I can't stand watching. I just want to get out of the house for a bit.

IAN   Are you all right for money?

BOYD   What do you think, without my first-team money? No, I'm all right.

PETE   Have they given you a date?

BOYD   They're looking at it again tomorrow.

PETE   You're walking all right. *(To Ian)* Isn't he?

BOYD   I'll go nuts if it isn't soon.

PETE   They'll tell you tomorrow probably. I mean you're walking much better. Isn't he?

            (WALCOTT enters. Stops.)

WALCOTT   All right, Boydie.

IAN   You can leave clearing up in here for a bit, Walcott. Go and give 'em a hand with the kit.

WALCOTT   OK.

            (He goes.)

IAN   How's Elaine?

BOYD   OK.

IAN   I'd have walked out if I'd been my wife when I had that sciatic nerve trouble. I'd have been off.

PETE   You get very self-destructive, don't you?

IAN   My mother kept bringing me these jigsaws and paperbacks.

BOYD   I just stay out.

IAN   I couldn't concentrate on 'em. You know those jigsaws you can get? The big hard ones with about half a dozen separate pictures in 'em. National costumes of the world. She kept wanting to know why I hadn't finished it.

BOYD   I get so violent, that's why I've got to get out.

PETE   Let's go and kick a ball.

BOYD   You know, I'm sitting there before she comes in, and I say right. This time, you're going to behave yourself, you're a bastard to yourself and, more important, you're a bastard to her.

IAN   You can't keep it up though, can you?

BOYD   Tiniest little thing. Nothing. No, I stay out.

PETE   Let's go and kick a ball.

IAN   Want to Boydie? Or aren't you supposed to?

(CLIVE **comes in and silently acknowledges them. They nod to him. He goes to the team sheet pinned up on the board.**)

BOYD   Come on then.

IAN   I'll see you out there.

(Pete and Boyd go. Clive reads the team sheet.)

IAN   Eddie just wants to have another look at Jerry Barclay.

CLIVE   What do I do?

IAN   You'll travel as usual.

CLIVE   You said the odd game.

IAN   I thought it was going to be the odd game. You were given the same opportunity, Clive.

CLIVE   Yeah, with Frankie Ford.

IAN   There's always another boy coming up behind. The conveyor belt doesn't stop because you've signed forms. You want that place, you fight for it. I think you can make it. But the pressure is on, OK?

CLIVE   My Dad's bringing . . .

IAN   I know; there'll be other Saturdays.

CLIVE   Last week I told him I was rested. What do I tell him now?

IAN   You haven't been dropped. No place is guaranteed.

CLIVE   He's six foot.

IAN   I'm six foot. That doesn't make me a goalkeeper. *(Going)* OK, Clive?

CLIVE   I haven't been dropped. I haven't been dropped. 'Course I've been bloody dropped. Why can't I grow?

(Exit Clive.)

SCENE 8   **Match day.** EDDIE **and** WALCOTT **by the team bench. Eddie is roaring out to the field, while Walcott, dressed in a smart tracksuit, warms up, bending and stretching. Floodlights.**

EDDIE   Vincent! Vincent! Keep him wide. Keep him wide. Jockey Him. Steve, fill in here!!

EDDIE, WALCOTT   *(Together, arms raised)* Our ball!!

EDDIE   Where do they find those referees? This man? This man! Cliff. Tackle! Good tackle! Chris, get forward now! Stop posing there! Shirley Bassey! Support! Support! OK, Walcott, get stripped. Vincent, move 'em up! Walcott, I'm putting you in on the right side of midfield. Close this man down, Cliff! He'll skin you! I want you to stop their number eight from crucifying us. Steven!! Like this lot have been letting him do all half. Now attack the box. Don't chicken out. Compete, Walcott, Pressure him, don't let him move an inch. Cliff, tighten up here! Here! Nice play, Martin. Nice.

EDDIE,
WALCOTT   Foul Ref!

EDDIE   Jesus Christ! Keep him on his right foot, Walcott! And compete for everything. He's earning three hundred quid a week, son. Vincent! Vincent! *(He raises a placard with a number four on it.)* If you can shut him out, Walcott, we've got a chance here. Now you go in there and show him you're the one who's worth three hundred pound a week. *(Ref's whistle)* OK, Walcott. In you go. Let's win, son.

(**Walcott stands with his hands up, jumping and loosening. Freeze. Crowd noise. Blackout.**)

THE MAKING OF THE PLAY

During the period I was writing for the Theatre Royal in the East End of London, a number of plays were performed there which centred on the lives and experiences of young people in that area. When Clare Venables, the Artistic Director of the Theatre Royal, asked what the next play should be about, I thought I'd suggest a subject that I'd wanted to do for some years, the *Football Apprentices*. She agreed, and suddenly I could go to watch football matches as part of my job. A dream come true.

Plays about football need large casts, and most small theatres can't afford to engage a large number of actors. However, the Theatre Royal had always attracted a good number of youngsters, both to watch the plays and to work there part-time back-stage and front-of-house. There were also some excellent drama teachers in the area who had organised youth drama groups which ran regular workshops. A mixed cast of professional actors and young amateur performers was therefore possible, but the agreement of the actors' Trade Union, Equity, whose job it is to protect the livelihood of professional actors, was needed to allow us to use a number of fifteen-year-old amateurs in the play. Fortunately, Equity was able to give its permission, and we started work.

Sebastian Born, a keen footballer himself, who was to direct the play, and I started to research the young footballers of London. We wanted to know more about this unpublicised area of professional football: the schoolboys being scouted, the apprentices themselves, of whom only one in three would ever make a living from the game, and the boys who find that, at the age of eighteen, they are released by their clubs.

We wrote to a number of London clubs and told them what we had in mind and asked for their help. (Those of you who might put on the play could write to your local club so that you could see for yourselves the work the APs do and the coaching they receive.) We were given assistance by Keith Burkinshaw and Pat Welton at Spurs, this at the time when Spurs were bringing Ardiles and Villa to White Hart Lane, and by John Lyall at West Ham. In the meantime, though, we had decided to set our club in the Second Division, so Sebastian spent most of his time at Fulham, and I at Orient. We watched, talked, made notes during summer training and the start of the new season. For the most part, we were like flies on the wall, just watching how the individual lads were progressing, their problems, their successes and failures in training and at matches, their relationship with the stars of the First Team. We also went to see parents, school teachers and schools administrators to find out their side of the story. Through this process, we came to have a greater understanding of the world of the football apprentices. We met in the evenings, and Sebastian would tell me what had happened at Fulham that day and I would tell him what had occurred at Orient. Scenes, incidents, dilemmas started to emerge; characters started to present themselves.

There were certain themes we felt we had to explore in the play. The most important one, I suppose, was what the club wanted from the apprentices, expressed in the phrase 'We want men at sixteen!' Also we wanted to explore the growing influence of young black players and the relation of this to the racialism of some fans; the crucial role of the parents, especially the dads, as their youngsters moved towards pro football; the relationship of the adults in the club to the kids; and the initiations which take a boy into the professional world.

When the play was in production, some scenes were filmed by the BBC (including the one in which Ian Anderson tells Frankie that the club no longer wants him) as part of a current affairs programme which explored what happens to the APs who are not signed on as professionals.

David Holman

FOLLOW-UP ACTIVITIES

Casting the play

Before a play can be put on stage the director has to cast the parts. He needs to find actors who look right, sound right and will be able to understand how the character they are chosen to play feels. A director cannot have a fixed idea of how the part will be interpreted because each actor will bring his or her individual interpretation to the part. However, it is still essential that the director has a clear idea of the kind of actor he is looking for.

For example, the first director of *Football Apprentices* wrote notes on each of the characters before he began to cast the play. This is what he wrote about Ian Anderson:

IAN: a young man, perhaps very early thirties, who has recently been playing pro soccer himself. A self-improver, he probably went on FA coaching courses while still a player. He is dealing with young players and their parents and may not always be sure of himself. He wants discipline and effort, and praises those who give it to him. One gets the impression that Ian's strengths as a player were hard work and determination. You can still see the player in him. Fit, strong, smartly dressed at all times. Has tried to improve his accent and his use of words.

Imagine you are the director of a production of *Football Apprentices*.

Write casting notes on the following characters:
    Walcott Burns   Pete Miller
    Clive Pope

Your notes should show what you think the character is like; what he looks like; what sort of voice or accent he will have.

It is sometimes helpful to think of examples of the kind of person you mean from among people or actors you already know. They could be people in your school or actors you have seen on television.

Designing the play
The first production of *Football Apprentices* was staged in a professional theatre with an old-fashioned proscenium arch. The set, which was designed by Gemma Jackson, looked like this:

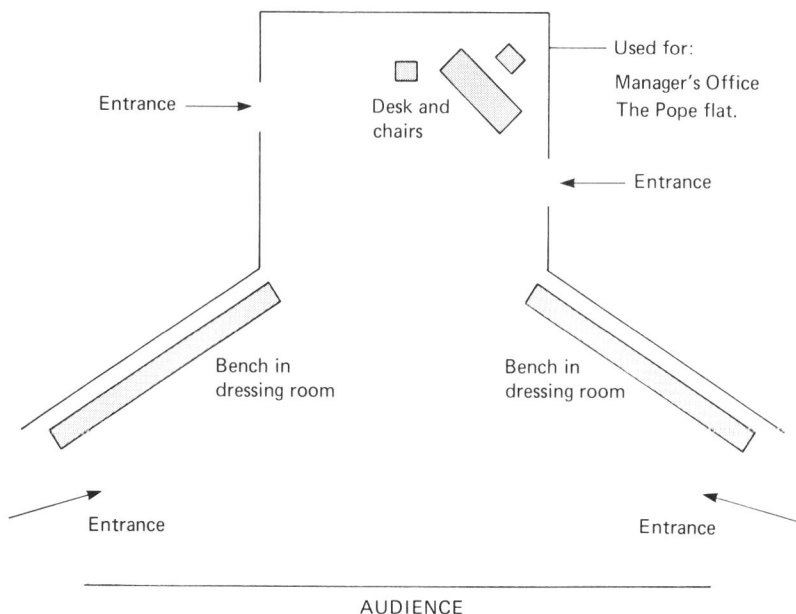

AUDIENCE

Black lines are screens

Here are two different theatre plans.

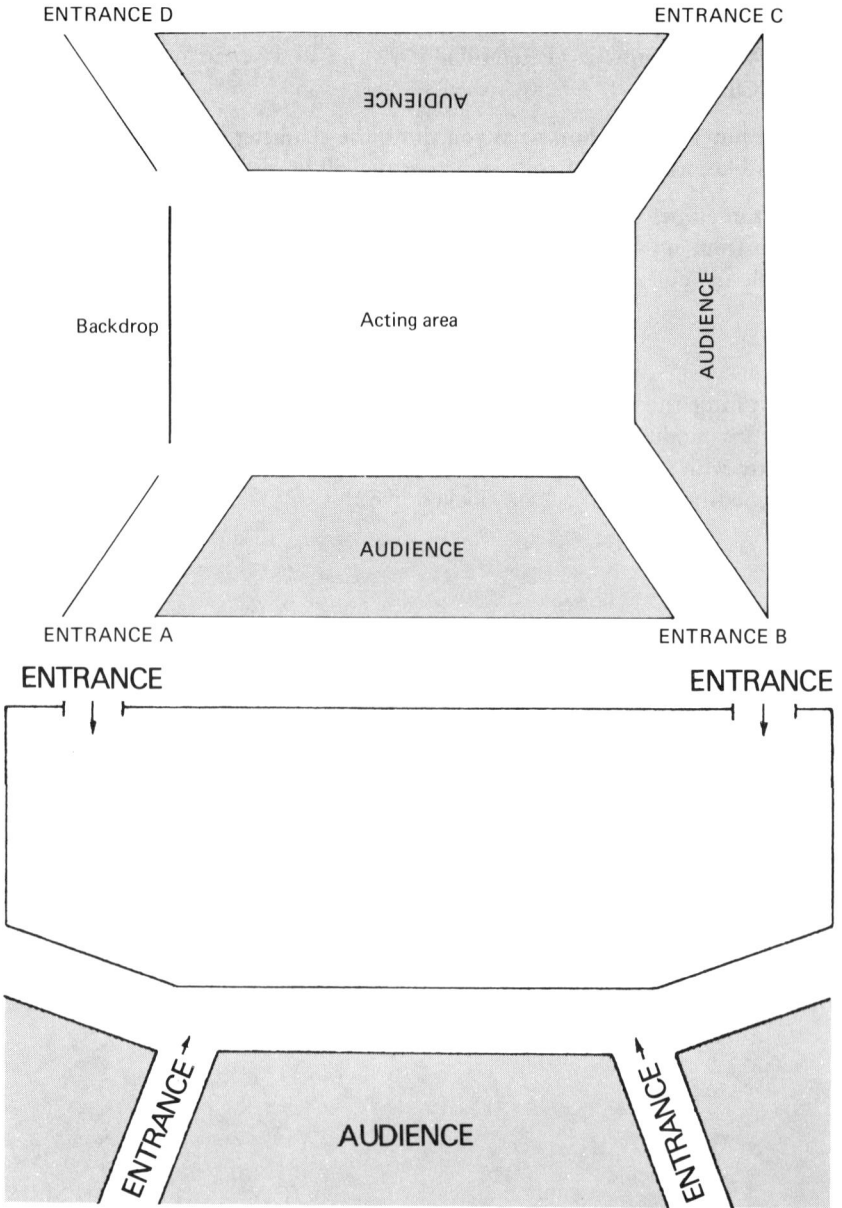

Can you design a set for *Football Apprentices* to fit one of these theatres? If you have a theatre, stage or drama room in your school, design a set to fit your space.

Designing the costumes

Here is how the costume designer working on *Football Apprentices*
planned Mr Pope's costume. She has drawn a picture of what she was
hoping Mr Pope might look like. She also wrote some notes about the
effect she was trying to achieve and the details.

It is very often the small details that make a costume 'work', especially
for plays set in our own time.

Select one or two characters from *Football Apprentices* and design a
costume for each. Try to make up some sketches. You do not have to be
able to draw, although it helps.

You could find examples of the clothes you are thinking of in magazines
or books.

For some characters you will need to do more than one design because
they change their costume during the play.

Make notes on the details: e.g. jewellery, badges, ties, etc. You could
include a few scraps of material to give an idea of what the clothes would
be made of.

If you are working on the costume designs of a real production, you will
need to give some ideas as to where the clothes might come from.

82

Editing and cutting

A play is not like a novel, which is completely finished when it is
printed. Because a play has to be interpreted by the director and the
actors, it is always changing. A playscript is a working document and the
writer, the director and the actors all have a right to change it if they
really think it necessary.

Here is a page from the original script of *Football Apprentices* after the
director had made his changes:

```
PETE      Not for me.

IAN       Pity. He was so good when he was fourteen.

PETE      He's never spent one minute of his life thinking about the
          game. His little brother Kevin's going to be a smashing
          little player though.

IAN       How old's he?

PETE      Eleven. I've seen him a couple of times over the marshes
          Sunday morning. In fact there's another kid in that side.

IAN       Talked to his father?

PETE      Yeah. Mr Marshall aint going to be pleased about Wayne
          though.

IAN       Micky Fielder?

PETE      Definite for me. Here, you know his uncle's got some
          connection with Stoke City? Delivers their pies or some-
          thing. He's Trying to persuade Micky's Dad to get him in up
          there. I think we ought to clarify things there. Quick.

IAN       Right. Clydie?

PETE      No he don't want to play football. He wants to be a vet.
          His heart's not in it. You seen that whippet of his?

IAN       Henry Holt. Got to have him.
```

Can you explain why the director made those changes? Has he improved the scene? What was wrong with it before he made the changes?

Are there any scenes in the play which do not sound right to you? Find a section of a scene which you think could be improved and make notes of the changes you think necessary.

Read your version to someone else. Does he or she agree that you have improved it?

Are there any sections of the play that you think should be cut out? Decide where your cuts would be and make notes on why you want to cut those lines out. Imagine you will have to explain to the author why you want to cut the play (David Holman spent a lot of time and effort writing those lines, so the reasons had better be good!)

Staging the play

The director needs to plan each scene very carefully. Not only will he plan the actions and the movements, but he will also have a general view of what the scene should look like and the effect it will have on the audience.

To do this he needs to ask himself a series of questions:

(1) From which entrance will each character come on and what position should he or she take up on the stage?

(2) At what points will each character move and how?

(3) Which objects and props need to be where during the scene?

(4) How can I be sure that the audience understands what is going on in this scene?

(5) How will I make the scene achieve its intended effect, e.g. funny or sad or exciting, etc?

(6) What do I expect from the actors in this scene?

Here is a page from the director's script:

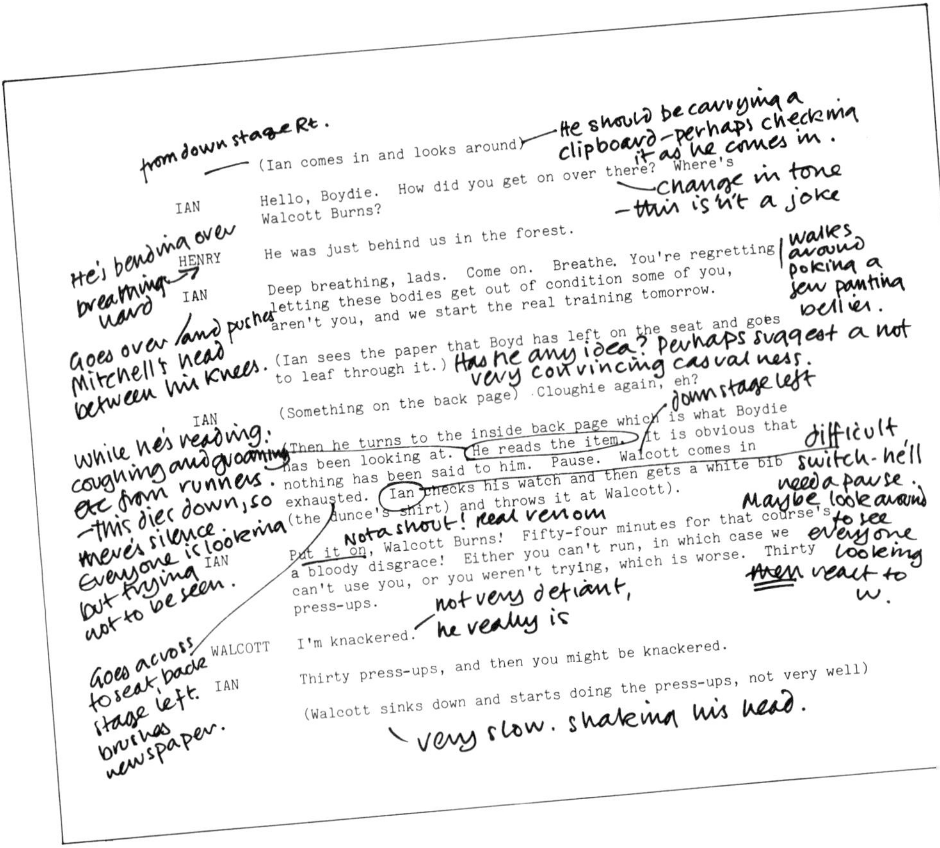

(Ian comes in and looks around)

IAN — Hello, Boydie. How did you get on over there? Where's Walcott Burns?

HENRY — He was just behind us in the forest.

IAN — Deep breathing, lads. Come on. Breathe. You're regretting letting these bodies get out of condition some of you, aren't you, and we start the real training tomorrow.

(Ian sees the paper that Boyd has left on the seat and goes to leaf through it.)

IAN — (Something on the back page) Cloughie again, eh?

(Then he turns to the inside back page which is what Boydie has been looking at. He reads the item. It is obvious that nothing has been said to him. Pause. Walcott comes in exhausted. Ian checks his watch and then gets a white bib (the dunce's shirt) and throws it at Walcott).

IAN — Put it on, Walcott Burns! Fifty-four minutes for that course's a bloody disgrace! Either you can't run, in which case we can't use you, or you weren't trying, which is worse. Thirty press-ups.

WALCOTT — I'm knackered.

IAN — Thirty press-ups, and then you might be knackered.

(Walcott sinks down and starts doing the press-ups, not very well)

from down stage Rt.

He should be carrying a clipboard – perhaps checking it as he comes in.

change in tone – this isn't a joke

He's bending over breathing hard

walks around poking a few panting bellies.

Goes over and pushes Mitchell's head between his knees.

Has he any idea? Perhaps suggest a not very convincing casualness.

down stage left

While he's reading: coughing and groaning etc from runners – this dies down, so there's silence. Everyone is looking but trying not to be seen.

difficult switch – he'll need a pause. Maybe look around to see everyone looking then react to it.

Not a shout! real venom

not very defiant, he really is

Goes across to seat back stage left. brushes newspaper.

very slow. shaking his head.

Pick one of the scenes listed below and work out how you would stage it on the set you have designed. (If you have not designed a set, look back at page 79 and use the drawing of the original stage plan.)

Practise making notes like those on the page above.

(1) Act One, Scene 1: the first part of the scene in the dressing room (pages 1-10).

(2) Act One, Scene 2: the first part of the scene in the classroom (pages 12-14).

(3) Act One, Scene 5: in the manager's office at the club (pages 30-6).

(4) Act One, Scene 8: in the dressing room at the club (pages 43-6).

Questions asked by the cast

During rehearsals, the play will be discussed in great depth by the actors and the director. The director is expected to have an opinion on most aspects of the play and will have to answer many of the questions asked by the actors.

Here are some of the questions asked by the actors who worked on *Football Apprentices*. How would you have answered them if you were the director?

Mr Pope

'When I come into the team dressing room in the first scene am I out of order? Are Dads normally expected to wait outside?'

'How good do I really think Clive is? Do I really believe Arsenal are interested in signing him?'

'Do I really know what I'll do if the club kick Clive out when he's eighteen?'

Ian Anderson

'What is going on in my mind when I finally get behind that manager's desk?'

'How difficult do I find my first decisions as a manager – the decisions about Alan Boyd and Frankie Ford?'

'What do I think of the new manager, Eddie Quinn? Do I think I'd be a better manager?'

Clive Pope

'What do I think of Walcott's football ability? How much better a player is he than I am?'

'What do I feel when Frankie plays such a bad game against Norwich? Am I pleased or what?'

'What do I think of my Dad? Do I really think he believes in me?'

Walcott Burns

'What do I think of Ian Anderson? I say some pretty insulting things about him. Do I believe them?'

'Was the serious injury to Alan Boyd my fault? If not, whose fault was it?'

'When Ian picks on me at the training camp it seems pretty racialist to me, but I never say anything. Why's that?'

Writing about the play

The follow-up work on the previous pages has concentrated on the process of presenting this play to an audience. Anyone who has worked on all the exercises is sure to have thought about the play in considerable depth. Any of these exercises will provide the basis for a longer piece of writing.

In school, however, it is often necessary to produce a longer piece of critical writing because that is the kind of writing examiners will be interested in. Here is a list of four essay titles on which to base a formal piece of writing about the play:

(1) 'We want men at sixteen.'

What does a club want from its apprentices and who benefits from this system in the long run? From what you have learnt about the AP system in this play, write about what is wrong with the system and suggest how it might be improved. (You could do this in the form of a letter to your local football-club management. If it works out well, send it off and see how they react.)

(2) Write about Clive Pope's experience as an AP. Show how he is influenced by the demands of his mother and father, his school and the club he wants to play for. In your opinion, do any of them really have Clive's best interests in mind? Can you predict what will happen to Clive in the next five years?

(3) David Holman says in his introduction (page 77) that he wanted to explore the 'growing influence of young black players and the relation of this to the racialism of some fans'.

How well do you think he does this with the character of Walcott? To what extent do Walcott's problems appear to be caused by his colour? In what way could David Holman have given us more information about the situation of black players in professional football? (You could write about this subject by writing some extra scenes for the play in which Walcott is confronted by the racialism of the fans and by the less obvious racialism within the club itself.)

(4) The BBC used part of this play to illustrate a documentary about football apprentices who do not make it as professional players.

Write part of the script for a documentary about the AP system. You should show how the system works, who benefits and who suffers. You could use Walcott and Clive as examples, follow their story and interview them about their experiences.